DOLLS' HOUSE
SHOPS, CAFÉS
& RESTAURANTS

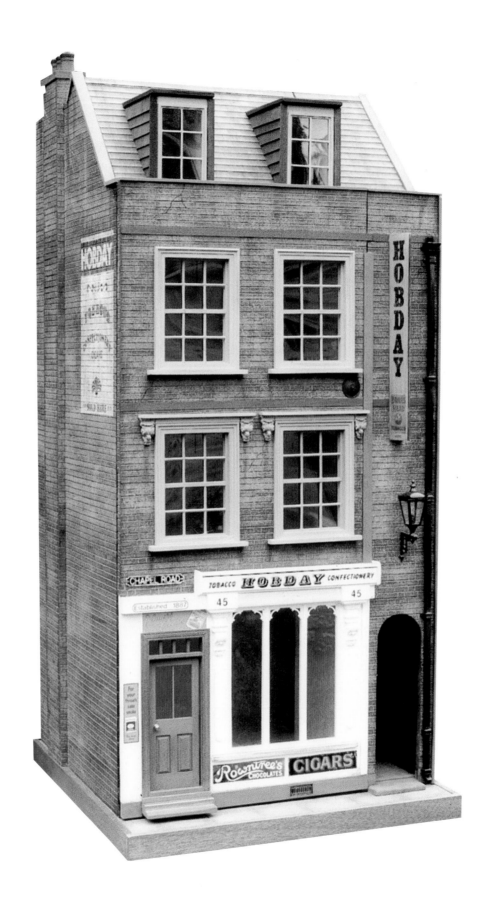

DOLLS' HOUSE
SHOPS, CAFÉS
& RESTAURANTS

JEAN NISBETT

Principal Photography by Alec Nisbett

Guild of Master Craftsman Publications

First published 2005 by
Guild of Master Craftsman Publications Ltd
Castle Place, 166 High Street, Lewes, East Sussex BN7 1XU

Reprinted 2006

Text © Jean Nisbett 2005
© in the work GMC Publications Ltd

ISBN 1 86108 455 2

Principal photography by Alec Nisbett
(Other photographic acknowledgements below)

Production Manager: Hilary MacCallum
Managing Editor: Gerrie Purcell
Project Editor: Gill Parris
Cover and book designer: John Hawkins
Illustrator: John Yates
Colour origination by Altaimage Ltd
Printed and bound by Sino Publishing House Ltd

PHOTOGRAPHIC ACKNOWLEDGEMENTS

Guild of Master Craftsman Publications gratefully acknowledge the following people
and agencies for granting permission to reproduce their photographs in this book.
The photographs on the following pages were supplied courtesy of:
P. H. Alden (Dolls House Holidays): 19, 26; Wendy Allin Miniatures: 34 ;
Jean Amos (photograph by Jeff Clark): 50 (top); Marie-France Beglan: 43, 49;
Carol Black (Carol Black Miniatures): 53 (top);
Valerie Anne Casson (A Touch of England): 15 (bottom), 30 (top), 48;
J. S. Collins (Gable End Designs), 13 (left), 23 (bottom right), 27 (top);
Bernd Franke: 46, 49 (top); GMC (Trigger Pond Doll Houses): back cover (left);
Ikuyo Hanami: back cover (right), 45 (top); Ann High: 17;
S. Hilbert (Chapel Road Miniatures): 13 (right), 20 (left), 21 (bottom), 51 (top), 52 (top and centre),
53 (bottom), 76 (top); M. P. Hostyn (Emily Art): 47; S. Jackson (Jackson's Miniatures Ltd): 42 (diagram), 62;
Lisa Johnson-Richards: 22 (left), 39, 58 (bottom), 92 (bottom);
Jackie Lee (The Dolls House Emporium): front cover, back cover (centre),12, 18 (top),
23 (bottom left), 27 (bottom), 28, 54 (top), 111;
Dominique Levy: 30 (bottom); Ray Lincoln (Lincolns of Harrogate): 15 (top), 42, 95;
Loi-yau Li (Loi's Mini Treasures & Workshop): 37, 38;
M. E. Messenger (Sid Cooke Dolls' Houses): 24 (bottom); V. F. Newey: 50 (bottom), 51;
George Parker (Elphin Dollshouses) 21 (top), (photograph of 'Annie Elliott' corner shop by Gill Green) 22;
Sue Popely (photographs by Wendy Allin): 43 (centre), 112 (top);
D. J. Preston (Dolls' House Workshop): 8, 24 (top), 110;
C. A. Rouch (Toptoise Design): 25, 112; Rika Sato: 45 (lower four pictures), 57, 142, 144 (top);
M. Sauter (Anglesey Dolls Houses): 20 (right), 44 (top two), 64;
Kathy Shaw (Imagine Model Making Ltd): (photographs by Tony Shaw): 28 (top), 38 (bottom), 40 (top), 41, 43 (top two);
Margaret Shaw (Delph Miniatures): (photographs by Tony Shaw): 40 (bottom), 52 (bottom),
41, 43 (top, two pictures), 52 (bottom); C. R. Taylor (Glenowen Ltd): 23 (top);
Paul Wells (Medieval shop model shown by kind permission of Natalie Clegg): 16.

**This book is for Guy, who shares
my interest in store and restaurant design.**

ACKNOWLEDGEMENTS

I acknowledge with gratitude the work of everyone involved with the production
of this book, and in particular Gerrie Purcell for her advice and encouragement,
my editor Gill Parris for her sterling work, John Hawkins for producing
such an elegant design and John Yates for improving on my draft diagrams.
Special thanks are due to the makers and suppliers who loaned miniatures
for our photography: Valerie Anne Casson, Sheila Collins, David Freeman,
Susan Lee, Nicola Mascall, Sue Popely, Zara Thomson Ribeaud and June Wright,
and also Glenowen Ltd, Margaret's Miniatures, Merry Gourmet Miniatures,
Caroline Nevill, Sid Cooke Dolls' Houses and Warwick Miniatures.
I am also indebted to the miniaturists who kindly loaned
photographs of their work to reproduce.
Finally, as always, I would like to say thank you to my husband, Alec,
for his time and expertise in photographing my own work and that of other miniaturists,
to produce so many of the superb pictures that illustrate my text.

A NOTE ON MEASUREMENTS

The standard dolls' house scales are 1/12 and 1/24, both originally based on
imperial measures: in 1/12 one inch represents one foot. Although many craftspeople now
use metric measurements, dolls' house hobbyists in Britain and especially America still use
feet and inches. In this book imperial measures of length are given first (with the exception
of materials that are specifically supplied in metric), followed by their metric equivalent.
Accuracy to the millimetre is generally inappropriate, and metric conversions
are often rounded up or down a little for convenience.

CONTENTS

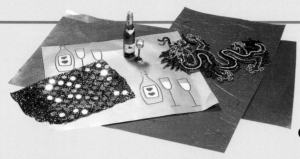

Introduction 8

PART I:
CHOOSING A PROJECT

Choices 12

Period-style Shops 16

Living Above the Shop 24

Specialist Shops 27

Clothing Stores 37

Four Boutiques 40

Food Stores 42

Continental Shops 46

Creating Atmosphere 50

Window Dressing and Small Shop Display Boxes 53

PART 2: CREATE YOUR SHOP

Decide on a Shop Style 62

Starting Work 65

A Single-storey Georgian Shop Kit 67

A Two-storey Shop 73

Ideas for Shop Signs 76

Decorate a Ready-built Shop 79

French Shop Decoration 80

PART 3: DEPARTMENT STORES

Emporia 92

Create a Store Department 93

Sports and Leisure 98

Ladies' Shoes 100

Gifts and China 102

A Food Hall 104

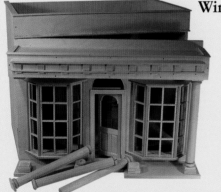

PART 4: CAFES AND RESTAURANTS

Eating Out *110*

Design a Café or Restaurant in a Room Box *113*

Changing the Look *114*

Eating Out – a Global Tour *120*

Dinner in a Georgian Assembly Room *122*

Visitors' Tea Room in a Stately Home *125*

French Café *127*

Café in a Conservatory *129*

Italian Ice-cream Parlour *131*

Spanish Coffee Lounge with a Moorish Influence *134*

Lunch in a Sydney Café/Bar *137*

Thai Restaurant *140*

Japanese Restaurant *142*

Chinese Tea House *145*

Indian Restaurant *148*

1930s Bar *150*

The Blue Dragon Club *151*

Suppliers *153*

Makers of Featured Miniatures *154*

Bibliography *156*

About the Author *157*

Index *158*

INTRODUCTION

In this book I take the dolls' house hobby beyond the familiar domestic setting of the 1/12 house, and show how, with a little imagination, shops, cafés and restaurants provide endless opportunities for the hobbyist. Whether you choose to reproduce period or modern style, you are sure to find a theme to develop in your own personal way.

My ideas for the book grew, in part, from early memories of shops I visited during my childhood and early married life. My first memory of a weekly shopping expedition was to a tiny, bow-windowed village sweet shop that I visited each Saturday with my friends. For the little we had to spend, we could buy a paper bag of 'sweeties' or two whipped cream walnuts.

Later on, a rare treat was to be taken shopping by a favourite aunt who had an eagle eye for antiques. We travelled to Leamington Spa, in central England, where the wide main street is still lined on both sides with elegant Regency buildings, most with shopfronts on to the street. At that time these included numerous antique shops for my aunt to forage in, and it was there that, in my teens, I bought my own first antique, a carved oak bookshelf.

▼ A sweet shop to revive childhood memories, with bay windows that allow plenty of space for an attractive display. The shop is available in kit form and, once complete, is 16in W x 16½in D x 29½in H (410 x 420 x 750mm).

▼ Also assembled from a kit, this fine antique shop has good proportions, an elegant façade and attractive windows. The basement can be purchased separately, in order to extend the number of rooms and provide a sidewalk area in front.

As a final treat, we always visited the town's department store, for that boasted the delights of The Palm Court Restaurant. There we had afternoon tea, with tiny iced cakes, and listened to the string trio of three elderly ladies, who played while seated on a raised platform edged with potted palms. Sadly, this no longer exists.

London's shops have always been considered the finest. In 1807, the poet Robert Southey was 'astonished at the opulence and splendour of the shops: drapers, stationers, confectioners, pastry-cooks, seal-cutters, silversmiths, book-sellers, print-sellers, hosiers, fruiterers, china-sellers – one close to another, without intermission, a shop to every house, street after street, and mile after mile …'

When I first went to live in London in the 1950s, I found the shops as amazing as he did. I remember buying gloves in an exclusive department store, where there was a gilded bentwood chair placed by each counter for the convenience of customers. To my secret astonishment, the salesgirl produced a dome-shaped velvet cushion so that I could place my hand on it while she gently eased on the gloves. How things have changed!

The little Georgian shop pictured on this page featured in my first book. Since then I have worked on many different shops, and each time tried to present the miniature stock to look its best. I soon found that one of the pleasures of arranging a shop display was that I could make changes whenever I felt like it, unlike the more static interiors of a dolls' house where I preferred not to move the furniture around too often.

I discovered the delights of miniature cafés and restaurants far more recently, and realized that this is a wholly different facet of the dolls' house hobby. The results of my efforts (and current obsession) are presented in Part 4, with a wealth of ideas for decoration and fittings to make.

Although many of the projects shown are my own, I have also called on miniaturist friends to contribute their own favourite settings, and craftspeople to provide pictures of the kits, shops and commissioned work for which they have become noted. There are examples of decorated shops from the rustic to the grand, and more homely interiors in shops and cafés, both period and modern.

I hope that this book will inspire you to make something for yourself, and to complete it in your own personal way.

▲ This was my first dolls' house shop. It was designed for a child to play with, and in the 1/16 scale generally favoured for that purpose. I enjoyed refitting this shop from time to time: it became in turn a drapery, an antique shop and finally a seaside shop specializing in nautical items, before being handed on to a child, as its maker had intended originally.

PART I

CHOOSING
A PROJECT

CHOICES

▲ This 'Marshall and Snellgrove' is a versatile shop with six rooms. It can be used as a department or general store, or as a specialized shop with living accommodation above. It is available as a kit, and can also be supplied decorated and with lighting fitted.

There are miniature shop styles to suit all tastes and all budgets: whether decorated externally; undecorated, ready for you to choose your own colour schemes; in kit form to assemble yourself; made to commission, or even – for the woodworker – as a set of plans to work from.

Ready-built shops and kits can be found at your local dolls' house shop, ordered through mail order catalogues, or purchased direct from the makers at miniatures fairs. Shop

plans are generally available through mail order. Look through the pages of your regular dolls' house magazine to source details of makers and selling outlets and to get an idea of prices, and look at makers' websites for more information.

The most expensive option is to commission a new shop. If you do this, you will acquire a unique piece designed exactly to your own requirements and finished in as much detail as you want.

Before you come to a final decision, bear in mind what you plan to put in your shop, and whether the miniatures will look best in a period or modern setting. Small shops are ideal for collectors of a specific category of miniature, to fill with china, shoes, food, hats, or whatever the chosen speciality may be, without the need to spend money to furnish an entire building – money that many hobbyists might prefer to use for additions to their collection.

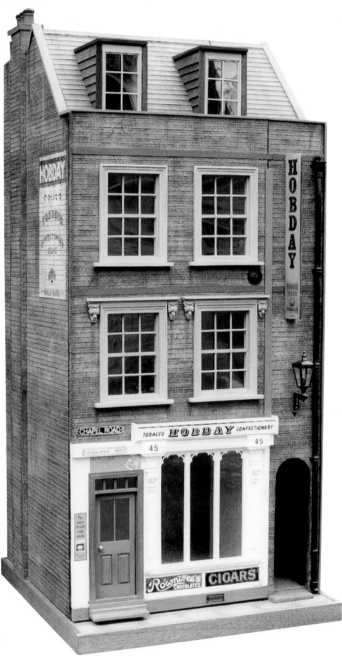

▲ This is a detailed model of a chemist's shop that is still trading in Tavistock, south-west England. It replicates the rather unusual form of weatherboarding and looks even better without the modern advertising that is now present on the windows of the real shop. It can be built from plans and a kit of fittings.

▲ A realistic example of a four-storey shop made to commission, with slate roof, brick cladding and authentic Georgian twelve-light windows. The Victorian shop front and door replace the original entrance floor of the building. (This shop is also shown on page 20, complete with contents.)

ORIGINAL DECORATIVE MATERIALS

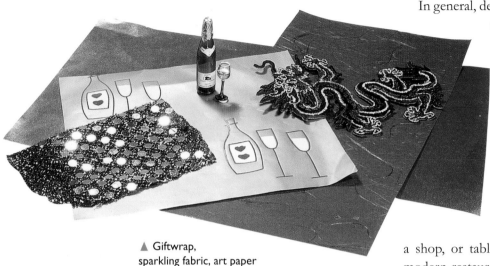

In general, decorations in shops and cafés can be more adventurous than in the conventional rooms of a dolls' house, and I suggest the use of inexpensive materials as wall and floor coverings, as well as those designed in 1/12 scale. There are also ideas on how to adapt commonly available objects to make, for example, display units for a shop, or tables and bar stools to suit a modern restaurant. Simple instructions and diagrams are included.

▲ Giftwrap,
sparkling fabric, art paper
and an iron-on fabric motif
to decorate a nightclub.

MODERN IDEAS

Most of my modern schemes were inspired by real shops, cafés and restaurants that I have visited and enjoyed, or seen pictured in magazines and travel books. Shop and restaurant design are both specific fields where the object is not to achieve the lived-in look that we would want for a dolls' house, but rather to provide an unusual and sometimes exotic environment to attract customers. Today's designers strive to outdo each other with new, inviting and sometimes amazing decor, and miniaturists can find inspiration whenever they go shopping or have a meal out.

◄ Simplicity is the essence of a modern Japanese restaurant catering for Western visitors: here there is a plain wooden floor and black lacquer table.

SHOPS AND SHOPPING

Shopping can be a chore or a pleasurable experience, whether it is a trip to the supermarket to buy food, or a more leisurely outing to choose clothes or furniture, or to buy a gift. Often it is the layout of the store that makes a shopping expedition particularly enjoyable.

In a miniatures shop, it is just as important to consider how it might appear to a customer as it is to arrange the goods in an attractive way, by leaving enough space between displays so that the interior will seem realistic.

Modern store interiors are included in later sections, as well as the much smaller but no less popular shops of earlier times. We begin with medieval open-fronted shops, continue with tiny, bow-windowed Georgian shops, then the general stores and corner shops that thrived in the late nineteenth and early twentieth centuries, and finally the colourful and spacious interiors of today's department stores.

▲ The carefully laid-out interior of this specialist grocery shop demonstrates how stock can be arranged to show everything clearly. The shop is fully lit and the shelving is adjustable to allow for packaging and goods in a variety of sizes.

CAFÉS AND RESTAURANTS

When we go shopping, we often pause for rest and refreshment before making further purchases. There are now cafés in book stores, where armchairs are provided so that customers can browse and choose books in comfort. Similarly, there are self-service cafés and formal restaurants in most large stores, and coffee bars in some smaller establishments.

This is not really a new idea: in London it was launched in the late sixteenth century, when a pastry cook opened a breakfast room behind his shop and, as a result, his business flourished at the expense of his rivals. In France, where food has always been important, a café attached to a shop was an early innovation.

I began to design and make cafés and soon decided to tackle more formal restaurants as well, ranging from the local bistro to the seriously grand; from the neighbourhood oriental restaurant to the Californian bar. 'Cafés and Restaurants' starts on page 109, but let's begin with shops.

◄ A typical French patisserie, where the baker stands outside proudly showing off his freshly baked bread.

PERIOD-STYLE SHOPS

MEDIEVAL

The first medieval shopping outlet was the market cross, a small, open, stone structure, ornamented with carving. Here the market traders could stand under cover to sell their butter and vegetables. Market crosses dating from the late fourteenth or early fifteenth centuries can still be found in cathedral cities

▲ A scale model of a particularly fine guildhall that was built in the early fifteenth century. This internal view shows, in the centre of the building, a massive brick chimney that would have provided some warmth on each floor.

▲ A model of a medieval shop, showing the shutter and counter arrangement that was commonly used in the streets of shops of this time. Today's 'lock-up' shop derives from this early beginning.

▲ The interior of a medieval merchant's shop, which the miniaturist based on historical details from manuscript illustrations of the period. The counter with parchemin panelling (an early version of linenfold) and the stepped dressoir (dresser) to display the pewter are handmade; the pewter goblets are carved from wood and then painted, and are indistinguishable from the real miniature pewter alongside, except by touch.

in the south of England, and are used today for the same purpose on market day each week. The carved detail on such crosses often includes angels to watch over the shoppers, a reminder that religion was central to the medieval lifestyle.

A guildhall would also have a covered space for market stalls below the rooms used as a meeting place for merchants or craft guilds, and sometimes the town jail was also in the lower part of the same building.

In towns, medieval shops were often open-fronted, and fitted with wooden shutters that in the daytime served as counters, and which could be lifted up and fastened securely at night. Each trade was concentrated in a narrow street, and the street names still survive in many market towns in England: Fish Row, Bread Street, The Shambles (butchers) and Cornmarket

are all names that tell us clearly where the medieval housewife – or her servant – did their shopping.

Wealthy merchants who dealt in high-quality pewter objects demonstrated their status to their customers by the shop building having glass in the windows, and by displaying their wares on fine furniture. Good security was essential and we can imagine that there were strong bolts on the doors and windows.

TUDOR

▲ A dolls' house version of a Tudor half-timbered market building with rooms above, inspired by Shakespeare's Stratford-upon-Avon.

The idea of a covered space for shopping at street level continued in the Tudor period. Like the guildhalls, many Tudor merchants' houses had such a space so that the market traders could shelter from the weather. This idea should appeal to you if you plan a shop but also want a complete dolls' house in the Tudor style.

◄ A Tudor town house with a space for small shops in the area below the jettied upper floors. The hand-carved wood, overhanging upper storeys and many-paned windows are authentic, and based on merchants' houses of the time.

This realistic figure of Shakespeare, a souvenir from Stratford-upon-Avon, is in the correct scale for a dolls' house or shop.

GEORGIAN

Shopping in the eighteenth and early nineteenth centuries was a popular pastime for people of means. The English novelist Jane Austen describes shopping expeditions made by characters in her novels, while her letters give an insight into her liking for pretty dresses, bonnets, ribbons and laces. She is said not to have enjoyed living in Bath, but her private letters indicate otherwise – she certainly enjoyed the shops.

Some of the shops Jane Austen visited are still in use today; they have elegant façades, many-paned bow windows, and usually a step up or down to the low doorway. In miniature scale, a Georgian shop is especially charming, and provides enough display space for a variety of small treasures. These shops were very small by today's standards, usually only one room deep, which makes such a single-storey shop a good project for a beginner.

▼ An attractive Georgian shop with Victorian alterations. The entrance door to the living accommodation retains its pediment, but the shop door now has a glazed panel in the upper part. On the other side, the original entrance for horses and carts is a realistic feature. The windows in the upper storey have lost their glazing bars and present a blank face to the street.

VICTORIAN AND EDWARDIAN

Victorian shops were larger than the Georgian ones, generally in two-storey buildings, and had the innovation of plate glass windows through which the stock could be seen more clearly from outside. Shop fronts often incorporated a tiled or marble entrance, and signs were more elaborate. These shops are popular with makers – who find them satisfying to design and build – and also with hobbyists, who can choose whether to use the above-the-shop rooms as storage or as living accommodation for the shopkeeper.

▼ A Victorian shop painted in the dark green often chosen in the nineteenth century. There is a private entrance door to the living accommodation.

▼ A Christmas scene is brought to life by the inclusion of child dolls. Signs indicate that this is a tobacconist as well as a sweet shop, a combination that is still prevalent today, in spite of the anti-smoking lobby.

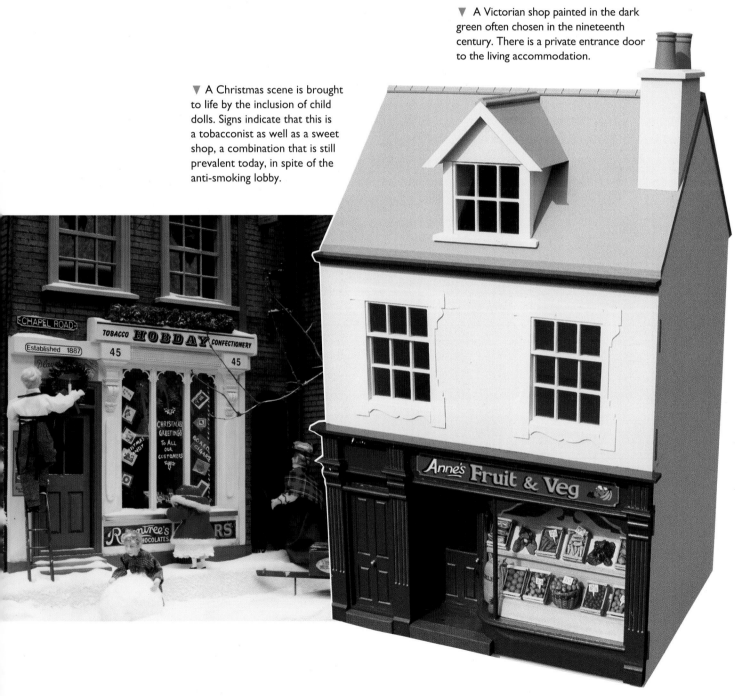

◀◀ Built and ready to decorate, this fine corner shop has working blinds and sash windows.

◀ A larger version of the same shop, with the addition of a working clock on the corner pediment, is shown fully decorated and fitted out by a hobbyist.

Above the shop, the rooms are used as living accommodation, while the two attic rooms are a bedroom and a workroom.

The corner shop flourished during late Victorian times and the Edwardian period that followed. Every locality seemed to have its corner shop, which sold a variety of things, ranging from groceries to household cleaning materials. Although many were owned by a solitary shopkeeper, others were part of a growing network of co-operatives, then and since known as 'The Co-op'.

Individual shopkeepers would boast proudly that they were 'Open All Hours', and indeed, in order to make a living, those in poorer districts did have to cater for customers who called in on their way home from work to buy food for supper.

A period corner shop can be arranged in a number of ways, to include a wide range of goods. It can become a greengrocer's or a baker's, an ironmonger's or a chemist's, or even a fish-and-chip shop, but in general it will be fairly downmarket, the sort of shop that would be almost exclusively patronized by customers from the immediate locality.

▼ The shop is the most prominent part of this building, although the living space appears quite substantial. The exterior, covered with period advertising signs and slogans, is fairly typical of the early twentieth century. The weathered brickwork is one of its maker's specialities.

MODERN TIMES

In recent times, once an area is 'gentrified', the corner shop – freshly painted and with gleaming windowpanes – is likely to become a craft shop or a children's clothing boutique, a bookshop or a flowershop, catering for the luxury trades rather than everyday needs, although some may still serve the essential function of being the local newsagent.

Another variation on the corner shop is a street of shops, or a row of houses with a shop at either end. To complete a project of this kind will keep you occupied for a long time, and the cost of fitting out and furnishing two shops and one or two house interiors could be spread out in stages.

Unless you plan to make most of the contents yourself, it is wise to estimate the final cost before you begin. Taking on a project that may prove too expensive is bound to spoil your enjoyment and, if funds for your hobby are limited, it might be better to tackle something smaller.

Provided the depth of several shops is similar, individual shops can be added one at a time to build up a row. If the buildings are of different heights, it does not matter, provided the scale looks right when they are placed next to each other, as in every shopping street there are shops of different periods and sizes. The trick is to make sure that a row of assorted styles will combine to make an attractive street. A very long street is perhaps best made as a group project by a dolls' house club.

▼ A boutique for children's clothing is a new use for the outmoded corner shop. For it to flourish, the area will have been colonized by better-paid couples with young families.

▶ Victoria Terrace is a realistic example of a house and attached shops in a northern English town. The maker has paid great attention to detail, from the carefully dirtied brickwork to the newly painted house door and the working blind on the end shop.

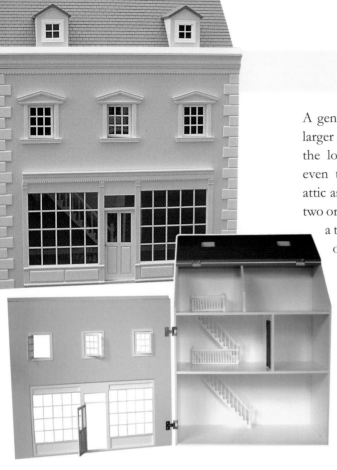

A GENERAL STORE

A general or country store is an altogether larger establishment – a shopping centre for the local community, and can be two or even three storeys high, incorporating an attic as storage space. It can be divided into two or three departments and may even have a tea or coffee room for the convenience of customers.

The general store can contain whatever you want: if sited in an imagined rural area it would cater for basic necessities like garden tools and gardening boots; but if thought of as sited in a prosperous country town, it could include clothes for the local county set and an interior decoration department devoted to handpainted furniture, gift items and pretty linens.

◀ A three-storey shop to assemble from a kit that includes an internal staircase, and an attic floor with a hinged, lift-up roof. It looks impressive but is simple to put together and has the added bonus that it is supplied ready-painted. Once you have assembled the kit, you can begin on the interior straight away.

▼ A country store that can be built from a kit, or supplied fully furnished. There are three rooms above the shop and a large attic. It measures 24³/₁₆in W x 14in D x 26³/₈in H (615 x 355 x 670mm). A lighting set and decoration pack are optional extras.

▼ A village house and store based on a Victorian original in Warwickshire, England, with an outshot to one side allowing space for extra storage. The window and double entrance doors are well integrated into the building and there is also a side door. The original was built to commission: plans and a kit of fittings are now available.

LIVING ABOVE THE SHOP

◄ Above the shop there is a cosy room for the shopkeeper.

▲ A baker's shop in a Tudor building with an updated shopfront is an original idea for a kit. The one-storey shop is available on its own, and the Tudor upper storey is a separate kit that can be added to provide living accommodation – or perhaps a café – above. The complete two-storey building measures 15¾in W x 14½in D x 17¾in H (400 x 370 x 450mm) and is made from 9mm MDF (medium-density fibreboard). As can be seen, the two kits fit together very neatly.

Until relatively recently, the shopkeeper often lived above the shop, where there were usually two or even three small rooms. Nowadays, this accommodation has often become a self-contained flat, while the shop-owner lives elsewhere, away from the town centre.

Many shops in British high streets are in old buildings where the lower part has been converted by adding a modern shopfront. Above the shop, the frontage may still be Tudor, Georgian or Victorian.

Makers usually base miniature house and shop premises on existing period examples, and the miniaturist is well catered for by such variety. Some diverse styles follow.

◄ A fine example of a Georgian house complete with a large ground-floor shop. It has a private side entrance surrounded by railings, and on the other side there is also a tradesman's entrance and more windows. Inside, double doors to the shop lead off a hallway. This is a large house and shop at 30in W x 19¼in D x 25in H (760 x 490 x 635mm), available as a kit or fully finished, and it is mounted on a turntable for all-round viewing.

A SCOTTISH SHOP AND HOME

Charles Rennie Mackintosh, the Scottish architect, designed just one shop, with a flat above. He received the commission in 1903, and was very pleased to have the opportunity to combine commercial and domestic functions in an imaginative way, while keeping to the traditional Scottish building style. When he designed these premises, he was already working on The Hill House for publisher Walter Blackie and also The Willow Tea Rooms in Glasgow.

► The solid tapering chimneys and the turret that follows older Scottish style are typical of Mackintosh's work. The walls are 'harled' (a Scottish form of rendering).

▼ Inside the miniature version, the maker has reproduced the generously proportioned shop floor space, while upstairs, the living rooms have handpainted wallpaper based on a Mackintosh design.

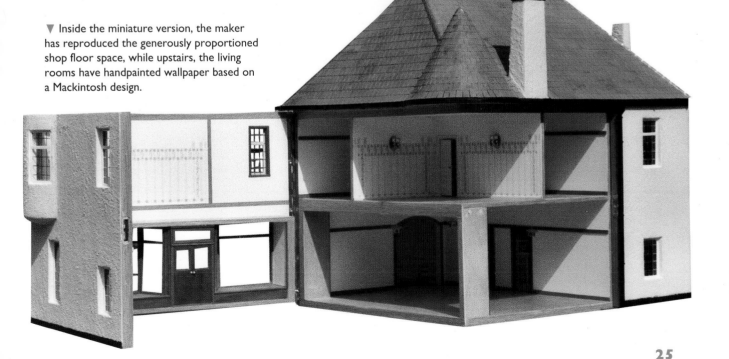

BUILD YOUR OWN SHOP AND HOUSE

Even those with little or no experience of house-building can succeed, given the right atmosphere and tuition. Here are two well-finished examples made by hobbyists taking a dolls' house holiday course; with careful instruction and supervision, they both achieved their dream shop with living accommodation attached.

These shops are based on a similar (but not identical) plan, but each was finished and decorated in an individual way. The variations in window glazing and framing bars, paint colours and cladding, give an indication of what the stock in each may be in due course.

▲ A corner shop with living accommodation.

▲ This hobbyist has completed a more ambitious corner shop with a house attached.

◄ A prototype design made as an example by the holiday course tutor; the windows and attic storey were used in the models made by the hobbyists. The Georgian door to the side of the shop and the cart entrance combine well with the Edwardian shopfront, in the manner of many updated buildings on modern high streets.

SPECIALIST SHOPS

A specialist shop might be stocked entirely with your own work. Whether you concentrate on miniature embroidery or needlepoint, assemble and paint furniture kits, make tiny flowers and plants, or paint landscapes, a shop to show off your achievements will be a delight to arrange. An added pleasure is that the stock will increase over a period as you complete new miniatures, so that this can be a long-term project.

Alternatively, you may prefer to collect miniatures by makers whose work you admire. Whether you choose a small or large shop, or make a setting in a room box to accommodate the miniatures, take care to decorate it in a style that will show them off to best advantage. For inspiration, the following examples include those made and arranged by professional miniaturists as well as some by hobbyists.

To start, here are two very different chemist's shops, one Canadian and one British.

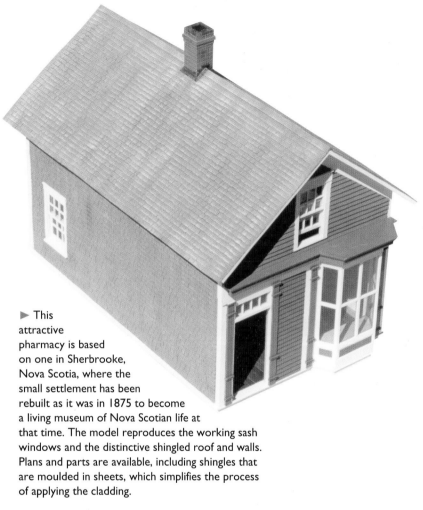

► This attractive pharmacy is based on one in Sherbrooke, Nova Scotia, where the small settlement has been rebuilt as it was in 1875 to become a living museum of Nova Scotian life at that time. The model reproduces the working sash windows and the distinctive shingled roof and walls. Plans and parts are available, including shingles that are moulded in sheets, which simplifies the process of applying the cladding.

▼ A chemist's shop set in an open-fronted display unit, based on the toy 'shops' that were so popular with Victorian children. This is a useful idea for the hobbyist with little space to show off a specialized collection. The unit is only 8¼in D (210mm), so that it can sit on even a narrow shelf. It is supplied with the shelves already assembled to fit onto the base. The counter is an optional extra.

INSIDE AN IRONMONGER'S

► This shop is based on one once owned by a great-uncle in the miniaturist's family, who was a boot and shoemaker, although here the range of goods has been extended.

▼ Everything is laid out very neatly in this ironmonger's. The customers are dressed in period costume, and the inclusion of carpet beaters, scrubbing boards, tin baths and many other useful items helps to give an impression of the hard work entailed in running a home early in the twentieth century.

One of the pleasures of creating a specialist shop relating to a particular period is to search out and display many of the objects that would have been commonplace at the time, in order to make a small record of bygone everyday life. Whatever you need to fill the shop, there is likely to be a miniaturist somewhere making what you want. In my chosen example, the inclusion of customers, obviously considering exactly what they need to buy, adds life to the scene.

In a realistic example of a traditional ironmonger's and general store of the type that has, sadly, almost disappeared from Britain in recent years, 'Fred Ogden' stocked everything you could possibly want for those small jobs around the house and garden. He could sell you six nails, if that was how many you needed, neatly wrapped in a twist of brown paper. Now you have to make a trip to the DIY store and buy a larger pack unnecessarily.

THE DROGUERIE

This version of a French hardware shop, in some ways rather similar to Fred Ogden's ironmonger's, was created by an English maker who now lives and works in Provence, France. The Droguerie dates from 1930, and the miniature version produces a powerfully nostalgic feeling both for the period and the region. The paintwork is distressed to look well worn, just like the original shop in the village of Cotignac, where it has become a tourist attraction.

The Droguerie features in guidebooks and on postcards. It is much photographed by visitors – so much so that the miniaturist sometimes runs holiday courses during which hobbyists can recreate their own souvenir Droguerie.

▼ Hanging on hooks, resting on ledges and spread along the narrow frontage there are ladders, brooms, baskets and tubs.

▲ The shop is 11in W, only 3⅛in D and 12¼in H (280 x 80 x 310mm). Just like the real shop, which seems to have been sadly neglected by its owners, it is crammed with a diverse and interesting stock – anything from hammers and nails to funeral items.

◄ The shop is open at the back so that the contents can be viewed from 'inside'. The window shelves are filled with an extraordinary assortment of pottery, kettles and even mousetraps. It is arranged in an apparently higgledy-piggledy manner but in fact was carefully thought out by the miniaturist.

CHINA SHOPS

Whether devoted to one type of china or porcelain, or to a mixed collection, china shops always attract admiring comments. The lower example shown here is the work of a French maker who specializes in miniature reproductions of nineteenth-century majolica. Her work includes teapots, jardinières, complete teasets and Strasbourg plates, all handpainted.

▶ Quirky animal and flower pieces are appealing, and look their best on a dresser, with enough space between each so that they can be looked at individually. The majolica is based on original pieces, but note also the traditional pair of Staffordshire china dogs on top of the dresser, betraying the fact that this maker is English although she has relocated to France.

▶ The delicate blue-painted shelves make a lovely background for this display. The room-box setting is top-lit, so that each piece, with its handpainted decoration, can be seen well.

FRENCH BASKET SHOP

A shop devoted to baskets is more common in France than in many other countries, where baskets have largely been replaced by shopping bags. In France they are used every day – particularly in country districts – to carry fresh vegetables, fruit and flowers to market. There are literally hundreds of designs, and these have inspired one English miniaturist now living in France to concentrate on this speciality.

The shop was made in America, but its contents were chosen and laid out to reflect the French tradition. The shop decoration and arrangement were done by the miniaturist's mother, who shares her daughter's passion for baskets.

▶ The shop is beautifully decorated with brick cladding and grey-green paintwork. The pretty cornice and the shop door are both painted white, to attract extra light. The stock has spilled outside on to the sidewalk.

▼ Inside, a glimpse of a casually arranged country shop, with bookshelves and a table for the shopkeeper, a shop till and, naturally, a basket chair. The brass door handle and lettering over the door add finishing touches. (See 'Ideas for Shop Signs' on page 76.)

▼ With the roof taken off, a bird's-eye view down into the shop shows the variety of baskets. The tiled floor, typically French, is tile sheet that has been carefully finished by adding grouting with a touch of grey colour so that it is not too new-looking. Tiny bunches of real lavender are a sweet-smelling addition.

TAPESTRY SHOP

I arranged this shop to show off the work of a miniaturist who specializes in the finest tapestry (needlepoint). There are cushions and firescreens, footstools and bell pulls in a gorgeous array of colours and designs. In the shop the pieces on show have been worked on various gauges of silk gauze, from thirty-four holes per inch to the very finest that can be tackled by the more advanced worker.

► The spaniel sitting on a tasselled cushion on this firescreen was one of the most popular of all Victorian designs. This example is worked on forty-eight holes per inch silk gauze. The cushion is one of a series of bird patterns in several different gauges which are available as kits.

▼ The stunning variety of designs on display are all based on original Georgian and Victorian patterns. Paler colours predominate in the earlier work, while during the Victorian period when Berlin woolwork became a craze, darker, richer colours were preferred.

This miniaturist occasionally works on an astonishing eighty-four holes per inch silk gauze, using an ultra-fine needle, to make special display pieces in 1/24 scale. All these designs are available as kits for you to work yourself, on different sizes of silk gauze. Whatever your skill level, if you enjoy tapestry there will be something that you can be confident you will be able to complete.

▲ The scallop pattern is fitted on to a mahogany Regency chair with fine ropework carving and a matching footstool, both by a specialist furniture maker who loves Regency and Georgian designs. The striking pattern, reminiscent of patchwork, is worked on forty holes per inch silk gauze.

▶ Full-sized carpets of this kind are made up in separate squares, which are then stitched together. This miniature carpet is edged with a 'ribbon' border and worked on thirty-four holes per inch silk gauze.

SHELL SHOP

► This little shop was inspired by La Ronde, in Devon, south-west England. An intriguingly shaped building, it was built in the eighteenth century for two sisters, who devoted much of their time to decorating every nook and cranny of its interior with shells. The miniature version is decorated with seaweed as well as shells.

This idea will appeal to anyone who likes to collect shells at the seaside, where, along with the more usual larger ones, there are always tiny specimens to be found – seemingly ready-miniaturized. If you are unable to collect them yourself, they can be bought in packs from craft and gift shops and sometimes at miniatures fairs.

You might also like to try making some 'seaside souvenirs' to go inside the shop, by gluing the very tiniest shells onto boxes to make a simple design and then varnishing them, as the Victorians did. The easiest way to glue them on is to use tweezers and superglue.

TOY SHOP

The secret of creating a really appealing toy shop is to arrange it with a child in mind, and imagine how a child would see it.

To achieve this effect, everything must be within easy reach of even the youngest child, as though ready to be played with.

► Filled with every sort of toy to delight a small child, this is a perfect example of a miniature shop. Many of the toys were made by the same miniaturist who decorated the shell shop, above.

AN ANTIQUE SHOP

An antique shop can be atmospheric, or carefully arranged to show off prized pieces. Given a distressed finish and arranged as a junk shop, it can be useful to store furniture that may be damaged or just plain shabby, but which you cannot bear to part with. Another use is as a temporary home for pieces that you plan eventually to use in a dolls' house or a more specialized shop.

My own antique shop offers a variety of ideas for interior decoration, with separate rooms to show off both specialized and general stock. Eventually it became so cluttered that I had to add another storey, taking advantage of an option provided by a number of makers who will supply a basement or an attic to add to an existing dolls' house or shop.

▲ China is one of the specialities of my antique shop, which includes Staffordshire figures, jugs and pots on a dresser, while smaller figures are on mantelshelves.

▲ Less cluttered than the room on the previous page, this part of my antique shop is arranged to show off unusual decorative objects as well as 1/12 scale furniture and glass.

► The Chinese excel at fine work. This miniature screen is an example from the Chinese mainland, where they also produce the pretty white wire furniture that is exported in quantity (see Chinese Tea House, page 145).

CLOTHING STORES

CHEUNG-SAM SHOP AND WORKSHOP

Anyone who has visited shops in different countries while on holiday or business will have been intrigued by the local, distinctive goods on sale and the ways in which they are laid out. In Hong Kong, the home of fashionable silk clothing and colourful, elegant shoes, the accent is on fashion combined with a working environment.

This cheung-sam shop and workshop – made by a Chinese miniaturist – is a modern-day shop full of beautifully made clothing and exquisite shoes and accessories.

▲ The miniaturist who laid out this shop says that cheung-sam is the most elegant traditional costume still much worn. In her first job as a teacher, she wore cheung-sam to school. The cheung-sam here were made by a tailor who usually works in full-size.

► An abacus to add up the bill is essential.

► The cheung-sam shop is a workshop as well as a selling establishment, with a sewing machine in the corner. The pin-up board on the wall above it has the details of orders to be made up.

Space in the shopping districts of Hong Kong is tight and the display space here is realistically crowded, giving a brilliant, jewel-like effect, quite different from a traditional Western store.

▲ The shoes, handbags and floral arrangement were all made by the miniaturist.

BOMBAY STORE

This shop is devoted to ethnic clothing. It is based on one in Britain, where some towns and cities have large Indian and Pakistani populations.

Sari shops are now a feature of British high streets, where the delicate, shimmering fabrics attract women in search of pretty evening wear.

► The delicate fabrics are all pieces of genuine sari fabrics. To add to the stock, the miniaturist also used plain cottons and decorated them with glitter-glue.

EDWARDIAN LADIES' CLOTHING DISPLAY

The elegant display in the Edwardian ladies' outfitter below is a complete contrast to the two previous clothing stores. The exquisite, handsewn dresses are shown on traditional tailor's dummies, together with large-brimmed hats, accessories and an array of hat boxes.

▼ The couture gowns and lingerie shown here are handstitched with great attention to detail, using the finest antique laces, ribbons and fabrics. The beautiful hats, wreathed with flowers, ribbon or trimmed with feathers, replicate original Edwardian designs. The miniaturist also made the decorated hat boxes, to protect the large-brimmed hats.

FOUR BOUTIQUES

Here and on the facing page are some unusual ideas for miniaturization that demonstrate how a well-designed setting can be enhanced by an imaginative idea.

Handbags were a great feature of Edwardian life but are now often just a part of the stock of a modern boutique. This stylish shop concentrates on leather goods – handbags and luggage, as well as another essential accessory, the umbrella.

◄ The smart modern façade of the shop immediately attracts attention. A neatly trimmed tree on either side adds a touch of class and the large shop sign is another eye-catcher.

This hair salon is an original idea that may be needed for a personal restyle after purchasing new clothes and accessories.

The miniaturist who created the salon had at one time worked in a hairdresser's, and decided to reproduce it in 1/12 scale.

► The dryers in the hair salon are handcarved from MDF, and there are plenty of realistic miniature accessories. The modern spotlights are a plus point.

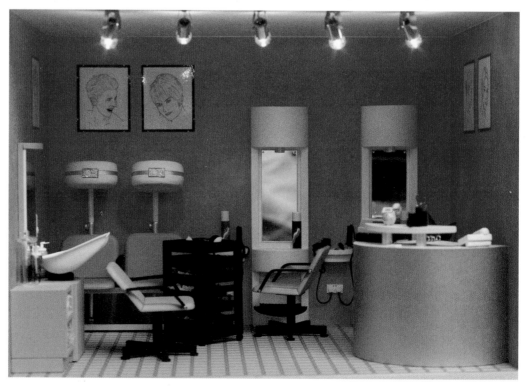

This is the shop to visit to find an original gift that might not be a priceless antique but will certainly have charm. Typically, much of the stock might be Edwardian, or from the 1930s.

A shop devoted to beautifully made furniture, whether period or modern, offers a good opportunity to the collector who enjoys furniture of a particular style. Chairs appeal to me especially, because I appreciate the skill involved in making them; in one department of my furniture shop there is my small collection of chairs, from Charles Rennie Mackintosh to Vico Magistretti, all made by miniaturists whose work I admire.

Mackintosh has enjoyed a resurgence in popularity in recent years and, in real life, reproductions of some of his furniture are eagerly sought by modernists. It has to be said that he designed seating furniture to delight the eye rather than for comfort, but in 1/12 scale, this will not be a problem!

▲ Treasures from earlier times fill this tiny shop. The pretty lace curtains at the windows and door reinforce the period feeling, while the sidewalk outside is used for oddments – and even a bicycle.

◄ This unusual shop is devoted to miniature replicas of Mackintosh furniture, produced by talented makers who specialize in his style.

FOOD STORES

▶ 'Simpkin & James' is a reproduction, to order only, of an old-fashioned grocer's shop, featuring traditional shelves and fittings. The Victorian cast-iron spiral staircase that can just be glimpsed through the windows leads to storerooms upstairs. This is a high-class grocer's that, in former times, would have catered for 'the carriage trade'.

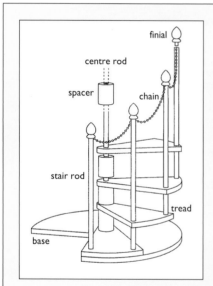

FIT A SPIRAL STAIRCASE IN YOUR SHOP

A spiral staircase is a decorative addition to a two-storey shop of any period. A simple version can be made from a kit that contains everything needed to put it together except glasspaper and glue. Instructions and a diagram are clear and easy to understand.

Food shops are just as much fun to tackle as a project as the more frivolous shops in the previous section. Choose a traditional, old-fashioned store or a modern delicatessen, and enjoy yourself filling it with suitable contents. If you are able to make food from a modelling compound you can provide most of the stock yourself, while a grocer's shop provides a good excuse to make packaging.

▼ The cheese and cooked meats corner of the Simpkin & James establishment, complete with marble-topped shelves and mahogany counter. This shop has been made to look like one where assistants take a pride in serving the customer.

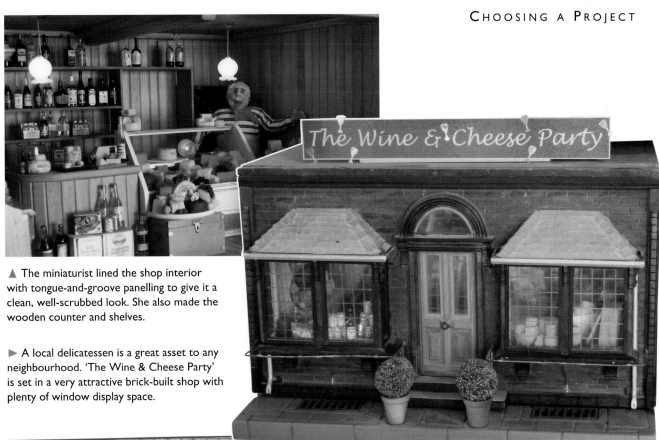

▲ The miniaturist lined the shop interior with tongue-and-groove panelling to give it a clean, well-scrubbed look. She also made the wooden counter and shelves.

► A local delicatessen is a great asset to any neighbourhood. 'The Wine & Cheese Party' is set in a very attractive brick-built shop with plenty of window display space.

◄ The cakes and bread in this baker's shop look good enough to eat, and the white scalloped pelmet with its neat trim emphasizes the clean and pristine look of this establishment.

► The schoolchildren excitedly waiting outside this French patisserie are impeccably dressed in period clothes. The dolls were made and dressed by a French doll-maker living in England, one of whose specialities is Edwardian dress.

A sweet shop may not be as essential as a grocer's or baker's, but for the miniaturist it can be as appealing as it might appear to a child. If you enjoy modelling food, you might find that making sweets could develop your skills in achieving the minutest detail.

◄ This little Georgian shop measures 15in W x 9¾in D x 9¼in H (380 x 250 x 235mm). It is one of a 'Mix-N-Match' range of upper and ground-floor units designed to be stacked.

A Sweet PLACE

► What a difference a coat of paint makes to the tiny shop. The vivid yellow would be sure to attract young customers.

► Examples of chocolates made by a professional miniaturist show that practice makes perfect.

▲ Greengrocer's

To end this section on food shops, here are some examples of Japanese shops made by two members of a dolls' house club in Tokyo. The neatness and presentation of the food in the greengrocer's, the delicatessen and the rice cracker shop exemplify the care that is taken with miniature work in Japan. Japanese are often short of space in their homes, and hobbyists choose shops as a speciality so that they can include as many items as possible. For this purpose, food shops are a good choice.

Every detail of these tiny shops seems to be perfect. Just as in full-size Japanese shops, great care is taken with the presentation of goods, which are always laid out carefully, and clearly labelled. Even vegetables are arranged in neat rows or bunches. Note the different roof styles on the exteriors of these shops.

◄▲ Delicatessen

◄▲ Rice Cracker shop

CONTINENTAL SHOPS

Miniaturists on the continent of Europe tend to favour decorative or nostalgic styles. Jewellery, costume and Christmas shops are particular favourites, as are cake shops which feature local specialities. The examples that follow – from Germany, Belgium and France – demonstrate the fine detail and finish that can be achieved by a skilled miniaturist.

A JEWELLER

Windows sparkling with gold, silver and precious stones are a magical sight, especially in the evening. In Germany, where this miniature was made, such shops are beautifully lit.

◀ The art nouveau frontage of the jeweller's is exquisite, while the interior, glimpsed through the shop windows, has been arranged to complement it perfectly.

BAKERY AND CAKE SHOP

This decorative shop stocks the stollen and gingerbread houses that are an essential part of any German Christmas.

▶ Bäckerei & Konditorei is decked out with a decorated Christmas tree and baubles, while a Santa Claus stands in the corner.

COMMEDIA DELL'ARTE SHOP

A Venetian carnival shop inspired the Belgian miniaturist to make something a little different from shops in her native country. If you travel abroad, it is worth looking at shops, cafés and restaurants to provide new ideas for your next project.

▲ This shop borders on fantasy and is a good example of the whimsical style favoured by its maker. The gilded decorations, the poster on the door and the shop name spell out its purpose.

◄ Inside, Colombina is crammed with masks, fans, feathers and filigree. The centrepiece is a tiny toy theatre complete with fringed curtain and proscenium arch.

LINGERIE SHOP

► The charming effect of this lingerie shop is enhanced by lifelike dolls looking into its windows.

The small shops below, made in France by an English maker, are a flower and gift shop and a lace shop. Both are stand-alone buildings, which are common in Provence. The flower shop also offers a range of related items and gifts, while the lace shop is a treasure trove of antique lace and vintage clothing.

FLOWER AND GIFT SHOP

▲ The flower shop is crammed with flower-related gifts including the table and chairs with unusual sunflower motifs.

► Provençal pottery is arranged on the table and dresser to catch the eye of any passing tourist; baskets are also a feature of these roadside shops.

LACE SHOP

▼ The interior of the lace shop, which also contains Provençal printed fabrics and neatly folded quilts.

► The lace shop is based on an actual shop in Provence.

All the shops featured in this continental section have their equivalents in other countries, and would be enjoyable to decorate and arrange in an individual way, but with the accent on the country of origin.

STALLS AND KIOSKS

Most people enjoy markets and, even today, when the enclosed shopping mall is warmer and more comfortable than a windy and possibly wet open-air market, there is no lack of custom. Many weekly markets in Britain have continued without a break since the thirteenth century when they were first granted a charter or licence.

Continental Christmas markets are famous, and for these the challenge is to create or copy a market stall that gives an authentic flavour of the original. The Christmas market trend has spread from Germany and Belgium, and such markets are now held in several UK cities, where they are proving equally popular. It might be worth checking out your nearest event next Christmas, to gain inspiration for your own miniature market stall.

► A German Christmas stall decorated with garlands and tree decorations. A snowy tree, gingerbread stars and trees, add to the realistic effect.

▼ This charming example of a French park kiosk is surrounded by realistic child dolls. The little girl dolls wear hand-smocked dresses, while the boy's sweater is hand-knitted.

◄ A Belgian Christmas stall that is fully enclosed, with a painted façade, glazed windows and a glass-panelled door. Inside there are toys, sparkling decorations and a decorated Christmas tree, while the cut-out Santa Claus on the door carries a snow-covered tree.

Parisian parks are green oases, sometimes with sandpits and swings, where children can play well away from traffic noise and busy streets. Generally there are seats and a kiosk where they can buy balls and small toys. I have seen similar kiosks in Japanese parks, but sadly they are rare in Britain.

CREATING ATMOSPHERE

▲ A lively Victorian street scene reminiscent of descriptions by Charles Dickens. The dolls are by leading specialists in their field and are all posed realistically. The scene was made to commission and the purchaser arranged the shops as a tea room, a clock and watchmaker's, and a pawnbroker's. Above the tea room there is a dressmaker's workroom, while the living quarters above the pawnbroker's are 'rather squalid'.

The majority of dolls' house shops are based on real period or modern examples, with beautifully painted façades and signs. The window glazing is clean and the shop interior will be arranged to look appealing.

But there is another facet to the dolls' house hobby: many miniaturists appreciate replicas of early shops that have fading paintwork, gently sagging roofs, fittings with visible evidence of wear and tear and stock that is not always immaculate. Fortunately, some makers cater for this and produce lovingly crafted, aged-looking buildings that reflect the alterations and dilapidation that would have occurred over the years to shops that first opened for business in the sixteenth century. Sometimes these atmospheric façades are linked together to develop into entire street scenes, and these often include a pub (bar) or tavern.

► A similar version of the same street corner and buildings. See how different it looks with atmospheric lighting but without people. The pawnbroker's shop is empty and the whole scene now has a slightly sinister aspect.

Even today, many shops in small towns and even large cities throughout Britain present a Georgian or Victorian frontage, with stucco or stone façades and sash windows. But many of these began as Tudor open-fronted shops, with shutters so that they could be boarded up safely at night. It was common practice in the late eighteenth and early nineteenth centuries to refront shops to look 'modern', and the updated façade will conceal low-ceilinged, beamed interiors and flagstoned floors that may be covered over by later flooring.

A market in London's Mayfair was not the most salubrious of neighbourhoods in the eighteenth century. Then, Mayfair was the haunt of prostitutes and thieves and only a brave person would venture there alone and unarmed. Shepherd Market was part of the Curzon estate, and it seemed that the noble owner ignored it apart from collecting the rents.

After it was leased by property developer Edward Shepherd, who built permanent market buildings, things improved. It is now an exclusive area, still with its own 'village' restaurants and specialist shops.

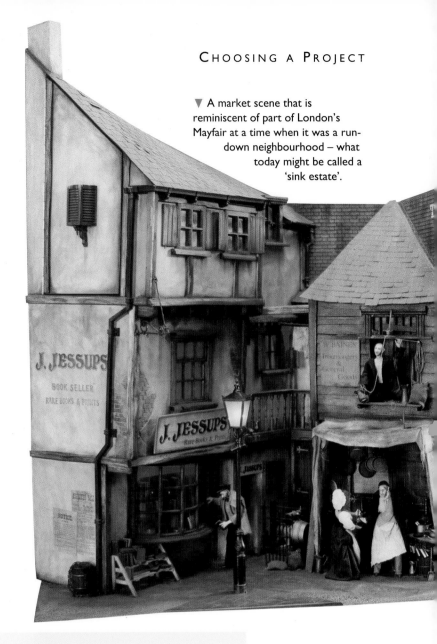

▼ A market scene that is reminiscent of part of London's Mayfair at a time when it was a run-down neighbourhood – what today might be called a 'sink estate'.

ENGLISH PUBS

Many taverns or 'drinking dens' had a bad reputation in former times, and were traditionally the haunt of thieves and highwaymen. Today, some of these remaining hostelries look picturesque and their built-up surroundings have become gentrified, but in the eighteenth century they might have been on lonely roads, away from neighbouring houses.

▶ Although The Black Bear tavern has a shabby exterior, the street light outside and warm glow from within make it look warm and welcoming.

► The Trinity Arms retains its original sash windows upstairs, but the brickwork has been freshened with white paint and new signs have been fixed to the walls.

▲ Another modernized pub, which is part of a brewery, looks very respectable. The weatherboarded walls are attractive, there is a large barred cellar in the basement and the name of the brewer is emblazoned on the front. You can almost smell the hops!

► In this pub interior, the glazed panel on the door and the stained-glass inset on the screen are typically Victorian. The wall telephone gives the game away – this is the modern version of an inn, decorated and provided with barrel tables and wooden settles in imitation of the older style. The wood panelling might just be original but today's developers try to include everything possible to mimic a style long gone that may appeal to patrons.

► A twentieth-century-style bar, although it includes a Victorian cast-iron pub table and a stool. This style has always been popular and is reproduced in many pubs.

For those hobbyists who want to fit out their very own pub, a good range of bar fittings is available. In an old-fashioned interior, you might want to install a traditional counter, made in mahogany, whilst for a modern bar you can include an up-to-date tap and refrigerated cooler cabinet. Bottles, empty or apparently filled, can be found in all shapes and sizes, with and without labels, as well as casks for the cellar.

WINDOW DRESSING AND SMALL SHOP DISPLAY BOXES

Window dressing is a specialized skill that can be learned. Do some research when you go out shopping: look carefully at all the shop windows and work out the features that help to make one look interesting and special, rather than dull. An eye-catching window is designed to entice the potential customer into the shop, and it is worth trying several different arrangements to make sure that your own display really would do just that.

Raised staging can be useful, so that items at the back of the window show well; the miniatures you use will determine whether there should be just two or three items, or a larger group. A good background is equally important as, just like a stage backdrop, it can be designed to emphasize the speciality stock.

▲ Even a simple window display can look stunning. Cranberry glass – a firm favourite in the nineteenth century and now very popular with miniaturists – is shown on the deep window sill of a shop with rough-cast, off-white walls, giving the display a country feeling.

◄ A realistic display of fruit and vegetables in a greengrocer's shop window. Shops like this generally extend their display on to the sidewalk outside, covering trestle tables with more boxes of produce and often with a metal bucket containing bunches of flowers.

WINDOW DISPLAY BOXES

▲ Brightly coloured flowers show up well in this small white display box arranged as a florist's.

Inexpensive display boxes measuring about 9½in W x 3½in D x 8in H (235 x 90 x 200mm) are available from several makers and many suppliers. These tiny boxes are, in effect, window display spaces: they consist of a ready-decorated façade with a glazed front window and a door that opens.

Some display boxes are fitted with shelves, leaving a narrow space behind for a few larger items, while others are left empty so that you can provide your own display stands of differing heights to show off the miniatures to best advantage. The back will be hinged and can be opened to allow easy access to arrange the contents, while the back wall can be used for posters or for further goods to be attached.

If you live in a small apartment or your rooms are all used by the family, it is not always possible to fit in a large dolls' house shop, but there will always be enough space for one or more of these shallow box displays, as they can be hung on a wall or stand on a narrow shelf – and it is surprising how many tiny treasures can be fitted inside.

Display boxes work best when used to hold a particular collection, as in such a small space too many contrasting pieces might look confusing. Once you have decided on a suitable background, all you need to do is to cut the chosen paper or card to size and fit it on to the back wall. It is also a simple matter to change such a backdrop.

I have tried out a range of different ideas in two styles of display box – one fitted with shelves and one without – to spark off your own individual arrangements.

BLUE-AND-WHITE CHINA

Restricting yourself to a single range or style, such as traditional blue-and-white china, ensures that pieces will not jostle for position, and the delicate pink-striped dolls' house wallpaper used here as a background does not overwhelm the fine china.

◀ A varied selection of pieces, no two alike, makes a display that is full of interest. If you want to display brightly coloured china, choose only a single type of pottery or porcelain, for example pieces based on the work of one designer, such as Clarice Cliff, or perhaps eighteenth-century-style pieces. A collection of figurines would look good, either in continental-style porcelain or more down-to-earth Staffordshire figures.

▲ A toilette set of ewer, basin and slop bucket, an inelegant name for a beautifully made miniature fitted with a cane handle.

▲ Harlequin and Columbine dance together in an exquisite porcelain double figurine, decorated with gold leaf. Porcelain figurines of this complexity are works of art, like the Chelsea, Derby or Meissen originals that inspire the maker; each has to be fired four times at different stages of decoration.

Take care when fixing prized china to display shelves. It is easy to cause damage if it is handled roughly. The best method is to fix a tiny blob of mastic adhesive (Blu-tack) to the shelf, and then press the piece very gently onto it. Never hold it by a handle or the narrowest part — always pick up the china carefully, holding the body of the pot. As every seasoned collector knows, porcelain figurines must be handled with the greatest care.

MUSIC

My music shop is filled with classical musical instruments and sheet music — a jazz selection would make a lively alternative. To cover the back wall, reduce a sheet of music to a suitable scale on a photocopier, or use musical giftwrap, which is usually available in a choice of colours.

▼ The cello and lyre music stand, made in mahogany and French-polished, make a fine statement at the doorway end of the shop, so that they can be looked at closely when the door is opened.

Musical instruments in 1/12 scale are generally inexpensive, especially the brass and wind, so that building up a collection should not cost a fortune. But it is worthwhile saving up for one or two superior handmade instruments as a centrepiece for your collection.

▲ I reduce-photocopied a few pieces of music to fold and scatter round the shelves. The narrow floor space behind is sufficient for larger instruments.

ANTIQUARIAN BOOKS

▲ The bookshop looks colourful and welcoming. Piles of books on the floor are typical of many second-hand bookshops where space is tight and the customers like to rummage.

▶ The quality of the printing and the illustration of this handprinted book is demonstrated clearly in this view of the frontispiece and title page.

following custom in some private libraries where the titled owner (not a great reader) filled shelf space with rows of fake books, bought by the yard.

A modern bookshop would also be appealing, and for this, pictures of new books can be found in booksellers' pamphlets or in magazine supplements.

As well as 1/12 scale books that cannot be opened, it is possible to include some printed miniature books that, although tiny, can actually be read (you might even come across one about restoring old dolls' houses that I wrote myself). Naturally, any special collectors' items should go at the front of the window display.

I find bookshops irresistible, especially second-hand or antiquarian bookshops. There is a particular, slightly musty smell inside, which signals the presence of out-of-print volumes, and the possibility of finding the one book that you have been searching for, sometimes for many years.

A miniature bookshop – without the evocative smell of old paper – is a nice idea for a speciality. I chose to miniaturize one that stocks old and rare books, and for this purpose used as the backdrop a leaflet showing shelves of antiquarian books that might be available at a book fair. Here, the shelves hold both specially printed books and inexpensive sets that come by the inch,

TRADITIONAL TOYS

▶ The mahogany finish of the display box has an old-fashioned feeling that provides a suitable setting. The shelf fitment inside is made of shiny brown card to resemble mahogany, so that the colourful handpainted wooden toys show up well.

Traditional toy shops that stock only handmade wooden and soft toys do still exist in country towns, even though today's emporia, filled with plastic toys and computer games, have largely displaced them. Miniaturists can still arrange and enjoy the sort of toys that would have delighted their grandparents, made and painted by dedicated miniaturists.

To advertise the stock, draw and cut out the letters to spell 'TOYS' on coloured card and fix them to a simple wallpaper background. The lettering need not be too regular, as it suits this shop if it looks as though drawn and cut out by a child.

If you plan a larger toy shop, you might like to use plastic letters designed for children's play – they are bold and colourful but in this setting would appear giant-sized.

◄ Toys made of pewter include a dolls' house and a carousel that can turn, while the tiny teddies are jointed so that they can be posed.

A HATTER'S

Most men these days prefer informal headgear or none at all, but there are still occasions when a hat is generally worn – perhaps for a wedding or at Ascot horse-race meetings, when a top hat is, for some, still the tradition. Countrymen need a cap and, until quite recently, city clerks in London wore a bowler, while in really cold weather an extraordinary assortment of headgear will re-emerge on the streets.

London's most famous gentlemen's hatters, Lock & Co., opened for business in the eighteenth century; the firm is still in the same premises in St James's, and is still

◄ The hats chosen for this setting mostly date from the early years of the twentieth century. There is also a selection to suit military customers.

patronized by those who want and can afford the best.

To catch the flavour of such a 'superior' establishment, the walls and shelves are plain and sober. They should not be too showy as they reflect traditional, conservative taste. The hunting-pink textured card is a good choice, but a plain mid-green would also be appropriate. It is important to get this right – too dark, and the hats would not show up well, while a pale colour could give a feminine effect.

◄ There is enough space behind the door to fit in a hatstand with more hats.

I chose to represent a long-established shop; any gentleman up from the country to buy a new hat should not be made to feel uncomfortable by any changes since his previous visit. The last thing he would want to see would be a new, modern interior.

▲ Admiral Lord Nelson and the Duke of Wellington both patronized Lock's for their military headgear, and there was apparently some rivalry as to who looked the most distinguished. The rifleman's shako from the same period is contrasted with a modern army cap, both made by the same miniaturist who made all the other hats.

◄ Surprisingly, some of these styles are still current stock at the exclusive London hatters, Lock's of St James's. The embroidered smoking cap worn by Victorian gentlemen and the check deerstalker favoured by Conan Doyle's 'Sherlock Holmes' are popular with American visitors to London to take home as a souvenir.

A MILLINER'S

A ladies' hat shop (or milliner's, in period style) would look equally good in a small window display box, but the background would demand a touch of feminine elegance. Choose a pretty but not too obtrusive wallpaper or fabric for the backing, and write a sign such as 'Hats Made to Order' or 'Millinery to Order' depending on the period, to place in the window.

► A selection of beautifully trimmed hats for the Edwardian lady. These elegant creations always completed an outfit, as no lady ever went out of doors without wearing a hat.

SHOES

My shop is based on one in our local market town, where traditional styles rather than high fashion are what many customers want. The shop caters for men, women and children, with shoes for country walks as well as the occasional evening engagement. There are slippers for cosy evenings by the fire, and pretty party shoes for little girls.

classic leather footwear

the Shoe lounge

▲ A sign always attracts attention, especially when it is linked to a special event in store.

The shopkeeper lines up the stock in neat rows, with no attempt at fancy window dressing, and the resultant display suits its setting. Everything is of the best quality, and local customers know that they will find exactly what they want. For me, this tiny shop display evokes a familiar scene.

▲ I used a greeting card, photocopied several times and pieced to fit the back wall, as a cheerful and very suitable background.

ADDING A SHOP SIGN

A shop sign may fit over the door, as it did for the Hatters (page 57), or inside on the back wall as in the Traditional Toys shop (page 56). A narrow sign can be fixed to the top of a window provided it does not obscure the display; small lettering is attached to the window of the shoe shop above, where it shows up well on the curved bow window.

the Shoe lounge

◄ Another option is to provide a freestanding sign board. For how to make freestanding signs and further ideas on signs and fascia boards, see pages 76–8.

PART 2

CREATE
YOUR SHOP

DECIDE ON A SHOP STYLE

Having looked at the examples of small and large shops earlier in this book, you should have a good idea of the style you favour, and also the type of goods that will be 'on sale' inside. You will also have been able to check out sample prices for the different categories at miniatures fairs, in dolls' house shops or in your regular dolls' house magazine.

You might even have spotted a dilapidated dolls' house shop on a market stall or in a second-hand shop and, if you enjoy the DIY aspect of the dolls' house hobby, plan to restore it yourself; this is a good first step before fitting out and decorating a new model, and the way I first learned how to repair and decorate dolls' houses. A more modern equivalent might be to bid for one on a computer auction site such as eBay. Whatever your preference, the numerous inspirational photographs included in this book will help you to make your choice.

BUILD A SHOP FROM PLANS

Most of the shops featured in this book are suitable for the dolls' house enthusiast who does not want to tackle advanced woodwork. If you have a woodworker in the family or have some experience yourself, you can buy a set of plans to make a bow-windowed shop plus living accommodation, complete with external doors and window frames, glazing, screws and hinges. You will need to supply wood, glue and tools.

For the more advanced woodworker, plans and some components are available to make the chemist's shops featured on pages 13 and 27 and the village store shown on page 23.

◄ One from a range of shops that can be built from plans. This version has a double bow window as well as a side window. Window frames, doors and doorframes made in styrene, which can be painted to look indistinguishable from wood, are available in both Georgian and Victorian styles as well as authentic period-style wooden mouldings and staircases to complete the interior.

ASSEMBLE A SHOP FROM A KIT

Like everything else, kit assembly becomes easier with practice. If this is your first attempt, begin with a room box or a small shop that will not be too demanding, as it is always encouraging to complete a first kit in a reasonably short time.

▶ It would be difficult to go wrong with this small, one-room Georgian shop, measuring 12in W x 10in D x 12in H (305 x 255 x 305mm). With its pretty bow window and curving pediment, it is an ideal first shop to assemble from a kit, for the hobbyist who has not yet made or collected many miniatures.

A SHOP OR RESTAURANT IN A ROOM BOX

For a beginner, a room box kit as a starter shop, café or restaurant may be a good choice (see page 100 where one is fitted out as a store shoe department, and page 145 where the same room box is used as a Chinese tea house).

Room-box kits to assemble (as well as completed boxes) are available from several makers and in a variety of sizes.

▶ A room box with side windows and a door provides an interesting interior in which to display the shop goods. The main part of this kit is of MDF (medium-density fibreboard), which slots together easily.

The kits can be plain and open-fronted, or have a sliding or lift-off glazed front; some may have a window or door on one side, while others have a top opening to provide extra light. They can be made of MDF or plywood, or sometimes include both – MDF for the main part and plywood for the trim, doors and window frames.

Both MDF and plywood need to have a smooth surface for decoration. MDF will need little smoothing but plywood should be sanded down carefully with fine glasspaper before painting or varnishing, and then be sanded again between coats.

Plywood room boxes usually have to be fixed with panel pins as well as glue, and these will be provided with the kit.

Kits made from MDF slot together into pre-cut grooves, and so glue is generally sufficient, but the parts should be clamped or held together with strong masking tape until the glue is set. Always try a dry assembly first, to see how everything fits together, before gluing the joints.

▼ A shop in a room box with a transparent top is another useful idea, so that the interior can be viewed from all angles.

STARTING WORK

Before beginning on your kit, think about where you are going to assemble it. A workshop is not necessary, but you will need a solid table – the larger the better. It is also a great advantage if you can set aside a room to work in, which does not need to be cleared up at the end of each day.

You will create some dust when sanding down, and will be using fillers and paints, so the table, floor and any nearby furniture must be well protected. A sink close at hand for washing brushes, and cleaning up generally, is useful and you will need good ventilation when using glues and paints.

TOOLS AND EQUIPMENT

You will need some basic tools and equipment for kit assembly:

A cutting mat

These are available in several sizes, from stationers and stockists of artists' materials. They are marked out with a grid of squares to aid measuring and cutting and will last a long time, as the surface is self-healing. I have two cutting mats, a large one to work on (and to protect my table) and a smaller one that I use when cutting small patterns in paper or card.

Ruler

An 18in long (450mm) see-through plastic ruler. Useful not only for measuring but also to check patterns on wallpaper before cutting.

Plastic set square

To check that corners are square when glued together.

Small hammer

Some kits require panel pins to be hammered in.

Screwdrivers

Kits with countersunk screws will have the holes ready drilled to take them. Check the type and size of screwdriver needed.

Masking tape

Use to hold parts together while glue is setting. It is generally cheaper to buy masking tape from an art supplier rather than a stationer, and you will be able to choose the width and strength you need. It will also be useful at the decoration stage.

Glues/adhesives

It is important to use the right glue for the purpose. Modern adhesives are not interchangeable. Very small shop kits (and also room boxes) may need glue only, and the maker may provide the glue. If not, use a wood adhesive (such as Evostik) to give a permanent bond, but remember that once set, the bond cannot be undone. A general all-purpose glue (such as Uhu or Bostik) will also be useful for joining small parts.

Remember that most glues give off fumes, so it is essential to work in a well-ventilated room, preferably with the window open. Keep strong glues away from children.

▼ A selection of basic tools laid out on a cutting mat

EQUIPMENT FOR DECORATION

Paint brushes

½in, ¾in and 1½in wide (12, 20 and 40mm) are the most useful when painting a 1/12 scale shop. I prefer to use relatively inexpensive brushes and throw them away when the shop is completed. Always start a new project with a new brush and never use the same brush to apply paint and varnish.

Artists' brushes

Sizes from 0 to 6 may all be useful. Do not buy the most expensive, as painting on wood will wear them out quickly. Brushes sold specifically for craft work are often intended for use by children and will not, in general, provide enough flexibility to achieve some effects.

Craft knife

Choose a knife with replaceable blades. If you are unsure how to change the blade, ask the supplier to demonstrate – mistakes can be dangerous.

Raised-edge metal ruler

Use this when cutting paper or card with the craft knife, so that the knife cannot slip and cut you.

Metal mini-mitre box and saw

To cut stripwood or wooden mouldings such as skirting board and cornice. Several makes (of a standard size) are available from model shops or dolls' house shops that stock DIY materials.

SAFETY FIRST

- Blades on craft knives must be changed frequently. They are inexpensive, and effective only when sharp – if blunt, the cut will not be accurate.

- To avoid accidents, always check before you cut that your free hand is behind the blade and not in front of it.

- Never use cutting tools when you are tired, as it then becomes all too easy to make mistakes. There is always another day.

- Always put a craft knife down while you check or adjust the position of the work. It is easy to forget that you are holding it and to nick yourself.

- Cutting tools are for use by adults only. Store a sharp blade safely by digging the end into a cork, and keep it out of the reach of children.

- Take extra care when cutting acetate sheet (for windows or see-through walls). This material is slippery and the knife can skid if not held firmly.

A SINGLE-STOREY GEORGIAN SHOP KIT

As an example of a kit (made from plywood) that is more complicated than the small shop shown on page 63, I chose a large single-storey shop in Georgian style. The shop is a good-sized 17in W x 11½in D x 14¼in H (430 x 290 x 355mm). The pillared frontage and architectural details on the façade are fiddly to assemble, but the result is worth the time it takes.

Detailed instructions and diagrams are provided with such kits, showing clearly how to tackle each step. This is a project that is suitable for a hobbyist with some experience, as there are many stages to the assembly. To build a kit successfully, make sure you follow the instructions, take care at each stage, and allow plenty of time. Never rush!

- Read the instructions in conjunction with the diagrams and check that you have all the parts.
- Then read through a second time, to make sure that you follow the sequence and understand how everything fits together.
- Try a dry run before you even think of gluing anything, and at this stage, smooth any rough edges with fine glasspaper.
- Most kits slot together easily but check that each section does fit exactly into the slot provided and, if not, sand carefully and check the fit again.

▲ The detailed façade dates this Georgian shop accurately to the early nineteenth century; the arcaded frontage made shopping more comfortable in wet weather.

► The open front seen from the inside. The overdoor panel will be painted, then glazed and fixed in last of all. The mouldings for skirting and cornice (not provided with the kit) are ready to paint, cut to size and then glue in after decorating the walls and ceiling and fitting flooring.

67

EXTERIOR DECORATION

Preparation

Once the kit is assembled, the surfaces will need some preparation before you decorate. It will be simplest if you deal with the interior as well as the exterior preparation at the start.

You will need:

- Medium and fine grades of glasspaper
- An emery board (as used for nail care)
- Interior filler

▲ When painting a pillared frontage like the shop used as my example, it is best to assemble and paint the pillars but not glue them into place until after the window frames are painted. The pillars stand on Blu-tack to keep them from smudging while the paint dries.

▲ An example of a window frame with a gap around it that needs to be filled and sanded smooth before decoration.

1 Smooth all surfaces, both outside and inside, with fine glasspaper, and fill any cracks around window and doorframes or between architrave and façade.

2 Paint with a quick-drying undercoat, both outside and in. Minuscule cracks may not show up until after the undercoat is dry, but could spoil the finished effect; apply undercoat over any filled cracks, otherwise the top coat of paint will not take properly on these sections.

3 Even if you plan to fix cladding to the exterior or wallpaper the interior, it is best to apply an undercoat to prevent any colour from the wood bleeding through delicate paper.

4 Finish the exterior with two coats of satinwood paint. If you want to pick out façade detail in a contrasting colour, leave for several days for the paint to dry out completely, then use masking tape to make a neat edge along the division between colours (see page 81).

5 Note that window glazing (fitted internally after painting the window frames) is not always provided with kits. Acetate sheet of a suitable thickness can be obtained from dolls' house and model shops or from stockists of artists' materials.

6 Make a thin card pattern to fit the window, mark it out on the glazing with a ballpoint pen, and cut the acetate with a craft knife, using a raised-edge metal ruler as a guide, or sharp scissors. Set the window glazing aside and fit after decoration is completed.

PAINTED EXTERIOR DECORATION

Two coats of satin finish (or eggshell) paint provide the simplest way to decorate a shop exterior. Painted shop façades look their best in one of the traditional colours used on real shops of their period. I chose to keep the decoration on my own shop simple, in keeping with the restricted colour palette of Georgian paint shades.

I made a sign for this shop to stand outside, as the architectural detail on the front of the building does not allow space for a fascia board below the superstructure. (See page 77 for how to make a freestanding signboard.)

The colour on the façade is a soft blue-green that was much favoured in the early nineteenth century, while the pillars, base and the main part of the shop building are painted as stone. To add interest, there is a line painted as stone just below the roof section.

You might like to choose from one of the modern paint ranges that reproduce historic colours: sample sizes are available to test out your choice. (For the more ambitious, ideas for a more elaborate exterior treatment are shown on the two-storey version of the same shop on pages 73 and 74.)

▼ The simple painted decoration is effective and suits the Georgian style. The flattened bow windows that became popular after the Napoleonic Wars allow a good view of the figures and flags inside.

COMPLETING THE INTERIOR DECORATION

This shop has a ceiling height of 11¾in (300mm), making the large room appear very spacious. The embossed ceiling paper provides additional interest and texture.

After the paper had dried out thoroughly, I painted it with an off-white emulsion paint to tone down the modern white of the regular wallpaper (a sample) that I had chosen.

INTERIOR ARRANGED AS A MILITARY MODEL SHOP

▼ A view of the inside, through the portico. Military lances on either side of the door emphasize the purpose of this shop. The gilded lion was bought from the gift shop at the site of Wellington's headquarters near to Waterloo.

This shop is large enough to be used for many types of retailer. I chose to use it for a military model shop, because I enjoy military models relating to the Napoleonic Wars. Previously my small collection had been displayed on open shelves, where the figures could easily be damaged, so I rehoused them in my new shop, which is the perfect size and the correct period style.

The panelled dolls' house wallpaper design, which I chose in a military-looking burgundy, suits the theme. The repeat pattern can present a difficulty when the panel spacing is not an exact fit for the width of the walls, and the best solution – for this example or any panelled design – is to use paper of the same colour as the background to cover the rear corners, where it will be less noticeable as infill.

▲ The shop windows have a good-sized ledge inside, providing plenty of space for a window display. The bronze replicas of Napoleonic figures and French guns are seen here from inside the shop.

▲ The panelled, burgundy wallpaper provides a suitable background for the military figures that will be included. The table with a gilded French eagle base (on the right) and the English version with an eagle that replicates carved wood will be the only furniture in the shop interior.

▼ Napoleon and his soldiers are on one side, opposed by the victorious Wellington and some of his soldiers on the other. A narrow woven carpet (in this case, a Turkish bookmark) divides the two. Similar carpet runners in 1/12, also woven in Turkey, are available from dolls' house outlets.

Centre the panelled paper on the back wall, leaving a small gap at each end if necessary, and start the paper on the side walls from the front edges. Mark on the walls the places where the panelled paper will end. Measure out the size of the plain paper necessary to fill in the gaps at the rear corners and allow an extra ¼in (6mm) on each side. Paste in the plain paper first, then the panelled paper with the same ¼in (6mm) overlap, so that there is no possibility of a gap showing up.

To be a true replica in 1/12 scale of the local military model shop that inspired my miniature version, the figures should, strictly speaking, be in 1/144 scale. However, military models come in many scales (but not the standard dolls' house 1/12). This is an anachronism that doesn't worry me and that my visitors never seem to be aware of. Relative scales are less important in a shop that may stock many different ranges of goods, than in a dolls' house where the scale of furniture and accessories should be consistent.

◀ A small replica of the Waterloo lion is on the marble table top, while above it, a reproduction of the famous painting of Wellington at the moment of victory looks suitably impressive.

◀ Although Wellington expressly forbade duelling amongst his officers, many possessed a set of duelling pistols. This miniature walnut case with a fitted interior contains a pair of flintlock pistols in the style of Joseph Manton, the renowned Regency gunsmith, and also shot mould pliers, cleaning rod, powder flask and even minuscule shot. The shot lid is ebony with a brass knob and the case is completed with brass hinges and a brass escutcheon plate. A truly remarkable miniature!

A TWO-STOREY SHOP

Here, the same shop is presented in a two-storey version – also available as a kit or ready-assembled – but the exterior of the building looks completely different. The decorations and arrangement of this shop were completed by a hobbyist who is skilled at paint effects, and enjoys arranging miniatures to look natural.

The exterior treatment of this shop is also authentically Georgian, but features brick cladding and textured stone paint, rather than the plainly painted finish representing stucco on my single-storey version. It is a more complicated way to achieve a good result, but very realistic.

◀ The façade is based on the traditional red brick and stone used in Sussex, south-east England, and also in New England in the United States. The shop logo between the first-floor windows neatly solves the problem of where to add a name when there is no space for a fascia board.

BRICK CLADDING

▶ A detail of the nicely weathered brick cladding.

Brick-effect papers are plentiful but vary in colour. On a period shop, choose one that resembles mellow, old brick rather than a modern, brighter colour. Buy enough to cover the walls plus an additional sheet or two to allow for joins and pattern matches. Check that all the sheets are from the same batch to avoid colour variation.

Cut a template for each wall from cartridge or brown paper and use this as a pattern from which to cut the brick paper. You will need to make neat joins in some areas, such as under windows and probably also above a doorway. Take care when cutting to ensure that joins in the brickwork will be

exact, so that you do not finish with part of a brick where the join meets another section. Glue carefully in place using PVA adhesive, and leave to dry out thoroughly.

To age the brickwork, paint the paper with acrylic or watercolour paints, using watered down black and grey to vary the tone and simulate grime and water stains, but be careful not to over-wet the paper. Practise on a spare piece of brick paper to achieve a suitable effect, and remember to darken the brick in areas where it would naturally become weathered. If possible, look at some real brick-built houses, so that you can see where this occurs.

INTERIOR ARRANGED AS A TOY SHOP

The plain, matt-painted interior, with planked – but not highly polished – wooden floors, is just right for a nineteenth-century toy shop and provides an uncluttered background so that the toys and rocking horses attract all the attention. Traditional toys predominate on the upper floor, and were carefully chosen to be in the correct period style.

An eighteenth- or early nineteenth-century toy shop would not contain anything like the amount of toys that fill today's shops and, like the Georgian house interior, decorations were plain and simple. Most children owned very few toys, and often they were allowed to play with them only on special occasions.

In Victorian times, commercially made toys became more readily available – even the young Princess Victoria had a very ordinary-looking dolls' house which was not specially made for her. If you plan a Victorian toy shop, it can be filled with colourful things to play with, and still include every child's favourite rocking horse.

▼ The handmade rocking horses are based on original designs. One has seats for two small children as well as the rider, while the slightly larger one is the right size for the posable little girl doll. Both rocking horses feature the bow rockers that eventually gave way to the swing mechanism that was considered safer (but was less fun to ride).

▲ On the upper floor, a scaled-down dolls' house is in Georgian style, and handmade wooden toys are displayed on wall-hung shelves. On the lower floor, model soldiers are on parade on the pine shelves, while books are within easy reach. There is enough space for four rocking horses, the speciality of this shop, without risk of collision.

IDEAS FOR SHOP SIGNS

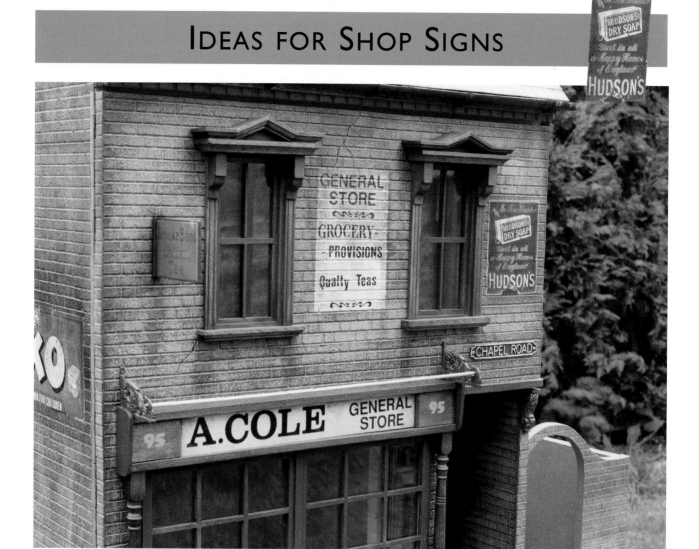

▲ In the Victorian and Edwardian periods, shop signs proliferated to an extent that would not be allowed today. Here is a realistic example of the signs that were commonplace then. They were mostly painted on metal to be fixed to the shop exterior walls, and dolls' house versions are widely available.

▼ Examples of freestanding signboards that are easy to make.

All shops, cafés and restaurants need a sign; it can be on the façade, over a door, on the window, hang from a metal bracket, or be freestanding outside.

The small window display boxes featured on pages 54 to 59 had no space for a fascia board, and instead I added small signs fixed to windows and doors. The easiest way to provide lettering for such a sign is to find a leaflet or advertisement that features a suitable typeface for the period of your shop, reduce photocopy it to the required size, and then mount it on coloured card. Alternatively, you can play with your computer to produce lettering in a suitable typeface and the exact colour and size you want.

MAKE A FREESTANDING SIGNBOARD

Another useful idea is to make a freestanding sign-board, like those shown on the previous page – I made mine out of thin (postcard-thickness) card. To suit the small size of the window display boxes, a sign about 1½in W x 2in H (40 x 50mm) will work well. This idea is equally suitable for a bigger shop (see page 69) and the board can be as large as seems appropriate.

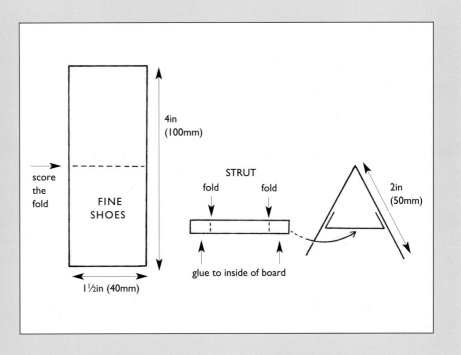

FASCIA BOARDS

A space is provided on many dolls' house shops for a fascia board. Suitable, well-spaced lettering is essential to give a good effect, and there are a number of ways to achieve this:

• Individual black letters on a white background can be found at most stationers and are self-adhesive. Fix them to paper and enlarge them on a photocopier if necessary before gluing them on to card and fixing the fascia board in place.

For the French brocante (see page 83), I was lucky enough to find some postcards depicting an early French alphabet in exactly the right size and suitable colour to cut and fix to card.

• The lettering on the fascia board on the French artist's studio (see page 87) was cut from a French magazine.

• Advertisements for French restaurants, which can be found in many countries, are another good source of ready-made signs.

• The brass-look letters on the Basket Shop (see page 31) can be bought at dolls' house shops that stock DIY materials. They are self-adhesive and need to be spaced carefully, but their raised profile and realistic brass appearance are striking.

Stencil a Fascia Board or Shop Sign

If you have tried stencilling and enjoyed it, you might like to use a stencil to create your shop sign. Inexpensive alphabet stencils can be found in stationers and shops stocking art materials in a variety of styles. Stencils will give a hand-finished look that is very suitable for a period shop or café.

► These examples were stencilled using a selection of marking pens. You will need to experiment on your chosen paper or card to see which type works best. On card with a glazed finish, a black laundry marker works well, without smudging.

► Some of the typefaces and colourways that can be produced by computer. Most computers and printers can now be set to choose from 'millions of colours', so there is no real limit to what you can do with colour and tone.

Spacing the Letters

Take care to line up and space the letters correctly. Fix narrow masking tape along the 'board' to make a base line, and similarly a top line, to fit the size of the chosen letters, so that the logo will be straight. Then work out the spacing by eye, allowing less space between thin letters such as I and J and more between fatter letters such as G and M. Practise first to make sure that you can achieve the wording you want, and trace the outline faintly in pencil before stencilling over it using a marker pen or paint.

Use a Computer

Probably the simplest way to create signs is by computer (technophobes: ask a friend or younger relation). Most computers now have a vast range of fonts to choose from, and with a little experimentation you can find the size you need. Letter spacing is automatic but word-processing programs usually allow you to reduce or increase the spaces between letters. You may also want to change the space between words.

Select the colour you require and, for the strongest effect, remember to set the printer to 'best'; 'draft' or 'everyday' settings offer a more faded effect that may be more suitable to give a period feeling. Photo paper, glossy or matt, or thin, coloured card (not too thick to jam in the printer) may work well, but as always you need some trial runs.

You may have a hundred fonts to choose from but, if you cannot find the exact one you visualized, it is usually satisfactory to accept the closest you can find.

The French shops that I have used as examples of shops to decorate in the next section have fascia boards. There are also examples of many different types of signs throughout the book.

DECORATE A READY-BUILT SHOP

To decorate a ready-built shop, follow the guidelines given on page 68 for initial preparation, undercoat and final decoration.

If you want to use more than one paint colour to emphasize beading around panels or architectural mouldings, it becomes more complicated. As examples of shops with plenty of detailing of this sort, I have chosen two small, two-storey French shops, designed by an English maker living in France, and created a French *brocante* (the nearest equivalent is an English 'bygones' or bric-a-brac shop), and an artist's studio and shop.

Decorating a shop front from a country that you may be unfamiliar with can be tricky, but most people have a mental picture of what they want to achieve. For additional reference, try looking at a travel brochure or guide books, where coloured pictures of typical shops are sure to be included.

▼ Design differences in the façades of these shops provide opportunities for decorative schemes with a French accent. The third 'shop' is now a café (see page 127).

FRENCH SHOP DECORATION

My colour schemes are taken from those widely used in France. Contrasting colours may be used in a variety of ways to emphasize the detailing, and masking tape can be laid to ensure a clean line between each section.

The shops are supplied ready to decorate and with copper tape wiring fitted, for those who like to install lighting. There are distinctive differences on each façade, but both have shutters and pediments that would be seen in the streets of French towns and villages.

The shutters are fixed in place (so that care must be taken when painting the façade) and the roof parapets are topped with a small ledge that makes painting inside the overhang of the parapet, with a steeply sloping roof next to it, difficult to access. In these shops the windows are ready-glazed.

The following hints show you how to avoid potential problems when painting these or similar façades, and so achieve a perfect finish. Apply these procedures to any shop that has plenty of detail, rather than a plain front.

◄ The shops are identical in plan: each has two rooms, with a non-opening door fixed to the back wall of each. Each measures 15¾in W x 8in D x 24in H (400 x 205 x 610mm).

AVOIDING POTENTIAL PROBLEMS

The Roof Area

To paint the inside of any parapet that has a small overhanging ledge, cut off part of the handle of a paintbrush to make it about 3in (75mm) long, so that you can more easily angle the brush into the tight space. Alternatively, packs of disposable 'bendy' brushes (with short, flexible handles) are available from craft and hobby shops specifically for this sort of job.

▶ This view of the roof on one of the shops clearly shows the narrow space between it and the edge of the parapet.

Fixed Shutters

Cut a groove along the side, top and base edges of a fixed shutter with a craft knife, in order to leave a small gap between the shutter and the façade. Masking tape can then be fixed to the edges of the shutter so that paint will not smudge onto it when the wall is topcoated. Leave for several days for the paint to harden, then repeat the procedure in reverse by attaching masking tape to the façade before painting the shutter.

Window Frames and Doors with Glazed Panels

Mask the glazing before painting the frames. It is quite tricky to lay masking tape accurately along each edge of window glazing and more so on a shaped door panel. Take your time and rub along the edge with a thumbnail, to make sure that the tape is stuck down firmly so that no paint can seep underneath. It is easier to achieve a perfect fit if you lay the shop on its back and place dark or black paper behind the windows while you work. When dealing with a glazed door panel that is curved on the upper part, you may need to apply the masking tape in short sections, trimmed to fit exactly.

▶ Masking tape applied to the glazed panel in a shop door avoids the risk of smudging paint onto the acetate glazing.

Unglazed Windows

If windows are not ready-glazed, bars will need sanding smooth before you paint them. To sand the small apertures, use an emery board (of the kind used for nail care), as this will be easier than using glasspaper in such a narrow space and just as effective. Smooth both before and after the surface is undercoated.

The Inside Front

The inside front will look best if it is decorated in keeping with the façade. I like to use wallpaper, but a painted finish will be equally acceptable. Most dolls' house wallpaper is a suitable size for internal room height; choose giftwrap or a regular wallpaper to cover a full height front without a join.

▲ An emery board is easier to use than glasspaper in a narrow space, such as the top lights of this shop window.

◄ The inside front of the *brocante* features a *toile de Jouy* patterned giftwrap in red and cream to complement the paintwork.

Each shop is very individual, and fitted out differently. For the *brocante* I chose a *toile de Jouy* patterned giftwrap, while for the artist's studio I used a regular wallpaper in cream with random blocks of colour that looked as though the artist might have painted them.

A BROCANTE

◄ A *brocante*, specializing in second-hand or antique furniture and accessories with a nostalgic appeal. Rattan blinds (glassmats cut to fit the windows) look realistic and contrast well with the rust-red paint so often seen on French shop exteriors. The fascia board was assembled from a postcard depicting an old French alphabet.

A tiled floor is an almost universal feature in a traditional French shop or restaurant, and is a good starting point to create the right ambience. A good choice is 1/12 laminated paper or card flooring, which is available as a sheet in a range of tile patterns and colours.

If your floor sheet has a border design, as mine does, it can be cut and pieced to fit the space. This is a simple matter with a geometric pattern to follow, and any joins between the border and the main floor area will not be visible after fixing in place.

The shop is fitted with regular-sized skirting board and a 'carved' cornice – fancy stripwood from the DIY store. The economical coloured glass 'chandelier' suspended from a ceiling rose is a non-working option, an inexpensive bead trimming from a haberdashery department. If you plan to light the room, suitable period-style lighting is widely available.

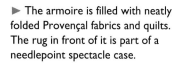

▲ This is an upmarket *brocante*, with the emphasis on antique rather than second-hand furniture and accessories. Above the shop, the salon is very grand.

▶ The armoire is filled with neatly folded Provençal fabrics and quilts. The rug in front of it is part of a needlepoint spectacle case.

◄ The bead curtain over the door is a reminder of France's colonial past. Porcelain, china and pewter objets d'art and a corner 'whatnot' with blue glass on the shelves make an attractive display.

▼ The elegant pagoda display unit fitted with glass shelves showcases silver and jewelled objects, while the wicker chair, with its petit-point cushion, looks inviting.

The stock needs to be a nicely judged mixture of antiques and bric-a-brac to tempt customers, so you need plenty of ornaments and objets d'art. Such a small room could easily become crowded, but wall-hung shelves and display cabinets can be supplemented by tables so that smaller objects can be arranged attractively without taking up valuable floor space.

THE SALON ABOVE

The room above my *brocante* is arranged as a salon in eighteenth-century French style. It is a rather grand living space, which suggests that the shop owners are fascinated by antiques from that period.

Provided you do not try to include too much furniture, an opulent effect works well even in a small room. In the salon, the tiled floor is giftwrap, the mouldings are gilded, and the gold brocade-effect wallpaper is a regular wallpaper sample. The French-style fireplace is in cast resin, and to add a further touch of grandeur, I painted both fireplace and skirting boards to resemble marble – an acceptable technique in even the grandest eighteenth-century rooms.

▲ The room is reflected in a gilt-framed mirror, while a matching picture frame holds a portrait of Marie Antoinette (cut from a postcard). The 'chandelier' is a glass bead trimming from a haberdasher's.

◄ The gilded sofa is covered in green silk with a gold pattern; on the low, marble-topped table, two wine glasses indicate that the room will soon be occupied.

TO CREATE FAUX MARBLE

A marbled paint finish can also be used on furniture, wall panels or pillars. It is easy to achieve on wood, resin or a wall surface and is quick to do.

1 Paint a base coat of cream satinwood paint or model enamel.

2 When the base coat is dry, add patches of a paler off-white, painting it on with a brush and rubbing off here and there with a clean cloth as you proceed, to allow some of the base coat to show through.

3 When the second colour is dry, use a fine brush to add veins in light grey, with a few smaller veins in brick red.

The marbling will look best if you paint swiftly and don't worry about being too exact – look at some pictures of real marble to judge the right effect.

▼ The decorative panel over the faux-marble chimney piece is a cutting from a French magazine; twist-stem glass candlesticks and glass and crystal ornaments add sparkle.

AN ARTIST'S SHOP AND STUDIO

The exterior decoration of my artist's 'shop' is based on Monet's house at Giverny in Normandy, so I decided to create a studio inside, where the artist could work and from which he would sell his paintings.

The upstairs windows on this model can be opened, unlike those on the other French shop, so that a garden dining room above the studio seems suitable. It is also a homage to Monet and other French painters.

I collected cuttings of paintings from magazines and art listings to feature in the studio. They are mostly French Impressionists, but not all, as I could not resist including a favourite painting by the eighteenth-century French painter Chardin, and a modern portrait by a Japanese artist working in Paris.

▲ The fascia board on the front of the building was taken from a feature in a French art magazine. The large window provides plenty of light and a good view of the paintings inside.

87

► The decoration of both studio and garden room was chosen to give a coordinated effect when the 'shop' is opened. Both rooms have plain, unpolished, planked wooden floors, while skirtings, doors and coving are painted in matt pastel shades.

The studio walls are painted in a pale creamy-yellow, and I photocopied the striking frieze from a book of Matisse prints. Matisse's famous cut-outs were a product of his old age, when he could no longer paint small detail but enjoyed cutting shapes and using them as appliqué. Amazingly, his agile figures were all cut freehand, with little preliminary drawing.

◄ The studio is shared by two artists and a sculptor; finished paintings are framed, while work in progress is mounted on canvases; preliminary sketches are pinned to the walls.

THE GARDEN DINING ROOM

▲ The French-style furniture is part of a ready-painted and inexpensive range from a mail order supplier. The Impressionist paintings on the walls are stamps from an exhibition, framed in narrow gilt mouldings.

◀ Masses of slightly overlarge roses, a bamboo blind and an ornamental statue add to the outdoor effect, and create the feeling of a French garden, demonstrating that it is possible to arrange a scene that might almost be outdoors in a dolls' house room.

▲ This armoire, without which no French dining room is complete, is filled with pottery made by a French miniaturist.

My garden dining room is based on one that still exists near to Monet's home in Giverny, where he used to meet his fellow artists for long lunches and conversation. A small studio in the garden outside is still there, neglected and shabby but very atmospheric, and quite different from his huge studio in the garden of his home. To create an open-air feeling, I used an embossed trellis-pattern wallpaper and added some delicate cut-out paper leaves as a border. As this is a home and workplace for an artist, the pictures tell the story.

89

PART 3

DEPARTMENT STORES

▶ Turn-of-the-century hat boxes and carrier bags, carefully made in extra-strong paper and card by a professional miniaturist, are suitable to contain hats or other more delicate items.

The first emporium (as they were known) opened in London in 1796, taking over a former ducal mansion in Pall Mall. The departments in the huge rooms were separated by glazed mahogany screens: there was a tea room on the first floor and workrooms above.

Harding, Howell & Co. lost trade during the Napoleonic Wars, and closed in 1820. In 1812 Swan & Edgar, a rival store, had opened in London. This was so successful that it continued in business until the second half of the twentieth century.

The new store was soon followed by others – the rise of the department store had begun. Perhaps the most astonishing development was the opening of Selfridges store in London's Oxford Street, in 1909. Selfridges is still a huge building, even by today's standards, but from the outset it rapidly established itself as one of the sights of London.

Gordon Selfridge introduced the American idea of including not only all the specialized sales areas but also every other

facility that the customer could possibly want: there were reading and writing rooms, a post office and an information bureau. In his advertisements he asked 'Why not spend a day at Selfridges?' and customers flocked to the store.

This was the start of shopping as an occupation for the middle classes, while upper-class Edwardian women remained loyal to smaller establishments, for a while at least. But it is also true that during the rise of the department stores in London and other major cities, Parisian shops were still thought to be more elegant, and fashionable and wealthy Edwardian ladies continued to order their gowns in Paris.

▶ Part of an Edwardian store display; it was a new idea to show clothes as they might be worn together, rather than laid out separately. The leg-of-mutton sleeves and high lace collar were the height of fashion, while a lacy parasol was a desirable accessory.

▶ An elegantly dressed customer who has enjoyed a successful day's shopping at one of the new department stores. Hat boxes were essential to protect the large-brimmed hats that were fashionable in Edwardian times.

CREATE A STORE DEPARTMENT

Shopping today has become an entertainment; large stores hold special exhibitions, demonstrations and promotional events on different themes each year to provide variety, and many older stores chose the Millennium to rethink both their layout and decor.

▼ Michelin House is one of the most recognizable art deco buildings in London, built in 1911 by the innovative Michelin brothers as a purpose-built tyre-fitting garage. Now, the front loggia houses an oyster bar and a flower-stall, and the major portion of the building is The Conran Shop, one of the most upmarket stores in London, devoted to everything for the home. This model is intended to be displayed on a shelf or mantelpiece and is smaller than the regular dolls' house scale.

The most noticeable feature of the update was often the building of magnificent new escalators. For the miniaturist in search of fresh ideas on shop decoration, a visit to a leading department store should provide plenty of inspiration.

Even the most committed hobbyist might not wish to tackle an entire store, although this is a splendid idea for a group project, where each member makes an individual department of their choice in a room box.

When assembled, the complete store is sure to attract attention at a miniatures fair or local exhibition.

A single store department is a rewarding individual project, and there are plenty of specializations to choose from. I have selected four departments as examples, inspired by the best of modern design – think of Harvey Nichols or the newly modernized Selfridges in London, or Bergdorf Goodman in New York.

▶ To make an escalator in 1/12 scale would need a great deal of ingenuity. It is simpler to use something that will look good when placed in the background, but without any moving parts. Here is one idea – a modern glass and metal rectangular vase.

TRADITIONAL SHOP FITTINGS

In an old-fashioned grocer's or baker's, you will want to include suitable fittings. For these, specialist miniaturists can provide period-style counters and shelving units that are perfect in every detail, while counters and display units are also widely available by mail order, and from dolls' house shops. But for the modern store, you may need to make your own.

The following tips apply equally to cafés and restaurants (shown in Part 4) as well as the department stores and small shops.

▲ A beautifully made mahogany shelf unit filled with delicious-looking cakes and freshly baked bread. Pull-out tray shelves are designed to hold bread rolls, scones and small cakes and buns. This could be the centrepiece of a traditional baker's shop.

IDEAS TO SAVE YOU TIME, TROUBLE AND EXPENSE

Small Boxes
These can be adapted to use as shop display fittings and counters, and also as serveries in restaurants. Keep any small boxes that come your way. It is also possible to buy inexpensive boxes with padded fabric lids that can be used as seating with very little alteration (see Banquettes, page 115).

See-through Plastic Boxes
These are useful as display units, as containers for bottles, or for protecting food in a café or shop setting (see page 139).

Artist's Mountboard
This is available in a wide range of colours and can be used to make shop and restaurant fittings. Offcuts can be found at a fraction of the price of an entire sheet and are usually large enough to make counters and tops for display units. Try your local picture-framer for these.

Double-sided Transparent Adhesive Tape (Scotch Tape)
This is less messy than glue and can be used to attach paper, card or fabric to walls and floors, or to fix a patterned or coloured top to a base unit. It can also be used to fix wallpaper onto a small area, where it is quicker to use than paste and avoids the anxiety of seeing wrinkles appear during the drying-out process.

Like masking tape (see page 65), it is cheaper to buy a large roll from a supplier of art materials, rather than the small ones from a stationer. The professional type is also much easier to use, as there is a peel-off backing; one trick is to turn a corner back after cutting, so that you do not lose the end.

Wallpaper
Dolls' house wallpaper is available in a wide range of period patterns but, when decorating a shop setting or a modern restaurant, a piece of full-size wallpaper with a carefully chosen design may be just as useful. Samples are often provided in a large enough size to use for a miniature setting, and are generally free.

Giftwrap
Similarly, giftwrap may provide a pattern that is exactly what you need. Sheets are large enough to cover the entire inside opening front of most dolls' house shops (see page 82) without a join. Even for a large shop or store in a room box, two sheets will generally be sufficient for most purposes.

Make a slide-in room liner to simplify decorating

slide-in liner (three walls)

use existing floor

slide in

Acetate Sheet

Transparent and coloured acetate is available in A4 sheets as well as larger sizes. Use it for window glazing, stained glass, or to add shiny colour to a café.

A Black Laundry Marker

This is ideal for signwriting (see page 78).

A Gold or Silver Pen

Buy the type that needs to be shaken up, then the tip pressed down firmly onto paper a few times to release the flow. These are also good for signwriting (see page 78) and for application to any small surface that needs gilding, for example picture frames. They save the chore of cleaning brushes after using gold model enamel.

A Set of Coloured Fibretip Pens

These need not be expensive: buy a set as supplied for children. Use them for colouring the edges of card or wood, to match the surface and so avoid showing a white streak where card has been cut. You can also use them to touch up any slight damage, or to match the edge of a wooden floor to the stain used. These are my favourite aid, as they can be used for so many purposes.

Keep a 'Bits Box'

A 'bits box' is invaluable. Store any attractive papers, cards, fabrics or ribbons that you come across. Greeting cards and pictures from magazines and even newspapers can often provide a painting to frame, or a small section of background, a lining for a cupboard or covering for a shelf. And as long as these are for your own use and not for resale (as all designs are protected for many years by copyright) you can have them photocopied larger or smaller to suit your purposes. Even if you cannot think of an immediate use for some small scrap, sooner or later you will find it will be just what you need.

▼ Cuttings from magazines and greeting cards and smooth and textured papers can be combined with dolls' house flooring to good effect. It is always worth saving decorative papers and pictures that catch your eye for future use.

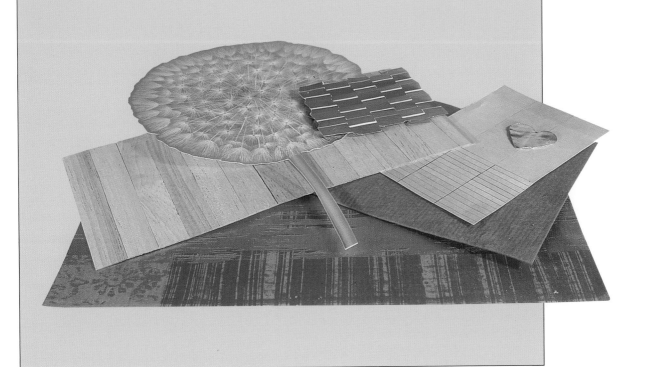

SPORTS AND LEISURE

▲ The handsome leather luggage display means that there is plenty of choice for even the fussiest customer, while the businessman can choose a briefcase for office use.

▲ A sporting print on the main wall emphasizes the nature of this department. Travel brochures (which came from an advertisement for holiday tours) are arranged neatly on the desk.

This department caters for sports enthusiasts and leisure activities. It includes a corner where customers can book a vacation, so it needed plenty of space to include sports equipment, leisure wear and luggage.

I made my own room box from foamboard, measuring 13¼in W x 12in D x 12in H (335 x 305 x 305mm). Very much a specialized men's department, it is given a suitably masculine feeling with the choice of a polished wood floor (in sheet form that is easy to cut and fit) and

plum-coloured paper on the main wall. One side wall is enlivened with a restrained spot pattern that picks up on the plum shade, while the other is a textured stone paper.

Plain furniture and units topped with plum-coloured paper to coordinate with the wall decorations give the right effect. I used both ready-made, inexpensive furniture and a low, pale wood box.

◀ A golfing set and clubs is shown next to a unit filled with leisure shirts.

ADAPT CHEAP FURNITURE TO MAKE MODERN DISPLAY UNITS

Don't neglect the possibilities of using furniture from a children's toy shop. Plain, pale wood is ideal for these display units and the desk for 'travel bookings', and it all came from a set of 'study' furniture that was inexpensive but needed a little improvisation.

To make the curved desk, I simply turned the 'study desk' back to front. A three-

drawer unit made two display units; the main part is used as open shelves, while the drawers from it are glued together laterally and topped with plum-coloured paper to match the walls. The wooden chair from the same set is a contemporary design; with the chair painted matt black and the support with aluminium model enamel, it is suitable for customer seating.

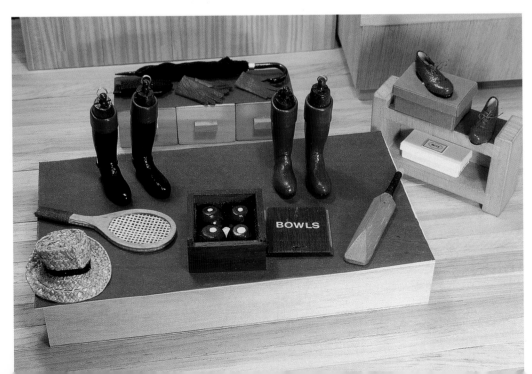

◀ The central display unit is a low box covered with plum-coloured paper. Riding boots for the country gentleman will attract the discerning purchaser. Made in the finest leather, they are provided with boot jacks to keep them in shape.

LADIES' SHOES

▲ The shoes, handbags and even the shoe boxes are all the work of one specialist maker, a master of her craft. A typical ladies' shoe in 1/12 measures only ¾in long (less than 20mm), is made of leather with a handcarved wooden heel, and fully lined. If only one were 5½in (140mm) tall!

Arranged in the room box discussed on page 63, the size allows for a varied selection of shoes and handbags for both day and evening wear. The setting is upmarket, so that it is obvious that only the highest quality designer shoes will be on sale.

The wallpaper is giftwrap and the flock paper used as carpet has a realistic appearance. To add to the luxurious effect, I chose a gauzy pale grey ribbon with silver edging to use as curtains but still allow plenty of light through the window.

▼ The pretty evening shoes, some with matching handbags, make a lovely display.

TO MAKE THE DISPLAY UNITS

Cover different-sized small boxes with silver card. The central unit, designed for customers to sit on while trying on shoes, is a circular plastic box that once contained soap. It is painted with metallic silver model enamel over a matt base coat.

Model enamel dries very quickly on plastic but will need a second coat to achieve a perfect finish. Don't be tempted to use a finger to test if it is dry too soon, or it may smudge badly.

To top the unit, cut a circle of dark blue fake suede (mine came from inside a jewellery gift box) and glue to the top to simulate upholstered seating. For accuracy, draw around a suitably sized round lid to make a perfect circle.

▲ It is important to provide some comfortable seating and the elegant sofa fits the bill perfectly. A long mirror that can be angled is essential, so that the customer can view the effect of different shoes with her outfit.

▼ This unit displays shoes for day wear, with matching handbags and even gloves. The hat was chosen to complement the red ensemble and add an extra splash of colour to the scene.

GIFTS AND CHINA

The gift department in a large store will be full of desirable objects – some of them may even be useful! This is where you can include almost anything you fancy as long as it is decorative, from artificial flowers and costume jewellery to china, cushions and silverware. You may also find a place for unusual miniatures that appeal to you but which are unsuitable for use in a regular dolls' house room.

The striking colour scheme is based on one I saw pictured in a book on retail design; the original is a boutique in Milan, Italy, but requires a different arrangement in a single-room setting, intended as a store department rather than a complete shop.

▼ The gifts and china department is an open invitation to buy: the miniature china, animals, 'silverware' and crystal included are all things that I was tempted by when I discovered them in similar shops or at miniatures fairs.

ADD TEXTURE AS WELL AS COLOUR

The textures of the wall coverings are as varied as the colours. A slightly textured deep tomato red on the side walls and the stone-finish thick card on the back wall look their best against the smoothly polished planked flooring, while the fake carpet in the centre 'aisle' leads the eye towards the main display shelf unit.

Although I had all the paper and cards in the colours I wanted to use for this scheme, the final arrangement was the result of much experimentation. Try moving display units around to see what will work best, so that all the stock can be seen and admired from the front of a room box. Once you are satisfied with the plan, re-check where each colour should go to give the best effect.

▼ The striking addition to the room above the yellow shelves was cut from a greeting card, and is actually a picture of a dandelion puff. In a store department, it is always a good idea to add some eye-catching large pictures or features to liven up walls and attract attention.

▲ A special display of miniature Herend animals takes centre stage on this side of the department, while the jewellery and 'silverware' has a gold-topped stand to emphasize its sparkle. On the wall above, tiny silk cushions are attached to a black foam 'board'.

China and porcelain always appeal to me; some of my collection features in special display shelves as the centrepiece of this room. The yellow box used for this once contained a miniature set of matching china, and the compartments were the right size to show off my own lidded jars and bowls.

The low unit showing glass and crystal is the lid of the same yellow box, while the other units are also boxes and lids. There is no need to buy units for a store department, as generally a suitable box can be found, although you may need to paint or cover it to suit the colour scheme.

▲ The crystal and glass miniatures are not dolls' house items, but are in a suitable scale. Artificial flowers in the corner are trimmings from a haberdasher's, while the Staffordshire china leopards are designed to suit a dolls' house mantelshelf.

A FOOD HALL

My final store department is a food hall, to give an indication of the beautiful fresh produce that we hope will be used in the meals provided in the restaurants and cafés in the next section of this book.

This is set in another large room box, measuring 17½in W x 13in D x 12in H (445 x 330 x 305mm), with enough space for a simulated escalator in one corner. The modern vase looks reasonably realistic in this setting, and reminds me of some of the futuristic escalators that were installed in department stores as part of Millennium refits. The advantage of this is that it can be removed temporarily, if I want to use it for flowers, as it is not fixed down.

▲ The food hall is modern and spacious and was based on the streamlined look of the Selfridges food hall in London. In the background, an approximation of a spectacular escalator is provided by using a glass and metal rectangular vase.

► Papers and cards used in the decoration of the food hall.

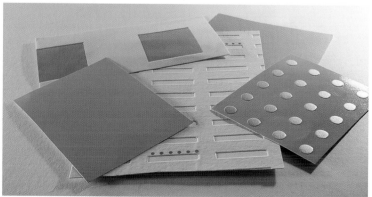

When creating a large food hall, make sure that you provide a clean, light effect and allow plenty of space between the units. White and silver are predominant in several of the papers in my food hall, and these make a suitable background, as colour will be provided by the food on the counters.

▼ The large round unit makes a focal point in the centre of the hall. Fish and freshly baked bread share an L-shaped unit, but are carefully divided by a strip of dried parsley to isolate the 'flavours'. A similar counter unit features in the Sydney café (see pages 137 and 139), but with a different finish.

MAKE AN L-SHAPED COUNTER

The size of your L-shaped counter may be varied to suit your own particular setting, but the measurements given below can be used as a guide.

1 Make the base by gluing two boxes together. The narrow end of the smaller box should abut one end of the long side of the larger box (see picture below).

2 Next, make the counter top from mountboard. It should be slightly larger than the base, to give a ½in (12mm) overhang on the front edges, but be flush at the back edges.

3 To complete the counter, cover the base and counter top with shiny coloured card, then glue the counter top to the base.

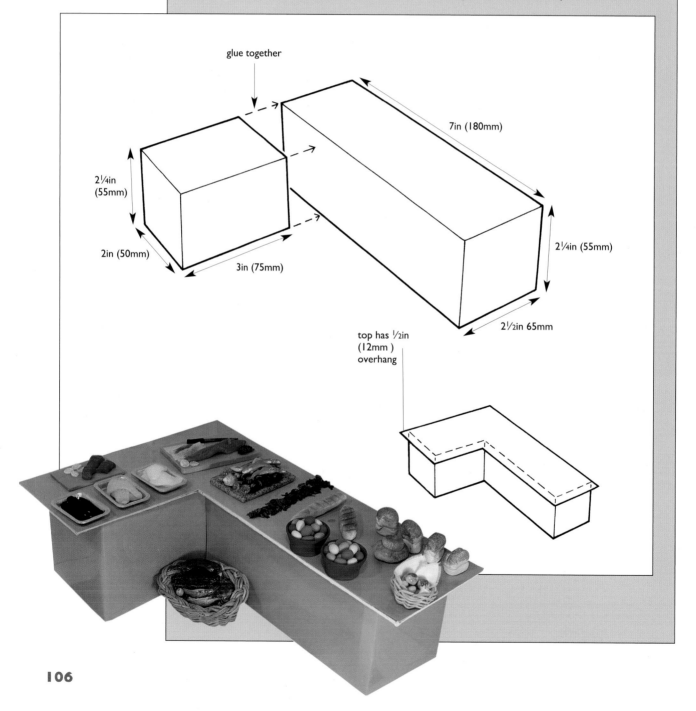

glue together

7in (180mm)

2¼in (55mm)

2in (50mm)

3in (75mm)

2¼in (55mm)

2½in 65mm

top has ½in (12mm) overhang

MAKE YOUR OWN FOOD

I used boxes to make bases for the food, and topped each with pale green shiny card to add to the cool, clean effect. All the food was professionally made but, if you enjoy making food from modelling compound, a food hall such as this might be the ideal place to show off your work – it could be added to gradually as you think of new fresh food to make. There might even be space to include a counter for chocolates and confectionery, or perhaps a stand in a corner for cookery books and magazines – or even a café or coffee bar.

◄ The round unit (a wooden box covered with shiny green thin card), is used as a counter for cheeses and cooked meats and pies. Round boxes in suitable sizes to make a base unit are widely available in gift shops.

◄ The fruit and vegetables on the counter were all professionally made and look very fresh.

PART 4

CAFÉS AND RESTAURANTS

EATING OUT

In real life, a special meal in a restaurant depends for enjoyment almost as much on the surroundings as the quality of the cooking. Reviews of new restaurants in magazines or newspapers always pay great attention to the style of decoration, and usually show a picture to give the potential diner an idea of what to expect in the way of decor as well as food.

▼ A nice example of the type of tea room to be found in most small towns and villages in Britain. The informal setting makes it the ideal local meeting place where friends can take tea and have a chat.

Inevitably, for the dolls' house hobbyist, this is all-important. Designing a miniature café or restaurant gives us a chance to try out schemes that would be unacceptable in a 1/12 scale domestic dining room, and to use colour and texture in different ways to create our own idea of an ideal setting for a meal out. Alternatively, you could base your scheme on a restaurant you have visited on a special occasion.

▼ Another familiar landmark is a local Italian restaurant, sometimes specializing in pizza and pasta, although there will be plenty of other dishes on the menu. This cheerful-looking pizzeria has been arranged in the same dolls' house shop that featured on page 23 as a country store, but with very different decorations.

SMALL CAFÉS

▲ This homely café is based on many in converted rooms over shops in small country towns.

Arranging a café is also a good opportunity for the miniaturist who enjoys dolls, as a few customers or diners will add a touch of realism. As an example, the hobbyist who arranged a realistic café above a north-country baker's shop has personalized the scene by including a customer and a formally dressed waitress; you just have to imagine the conversation!

I also like the idea of a café next to a shop; the one shown is based on a Scottish post office-cum-general store, where the mail box is set into the wall of the building. Opportunities for eating outdoors in Britain are limited because of the rainy climate, but when the sun does appear it is an enjoyable experience.

On page 118 there is an idea for a larger café set in a garden centre, where plants and flowers are used to make a colourful courtyard.

► The post office store has extended to provide refreshments next to the shop. Until recent closures, local post offices across Britain also functioned as general stores and stationers as well as general meeting places.

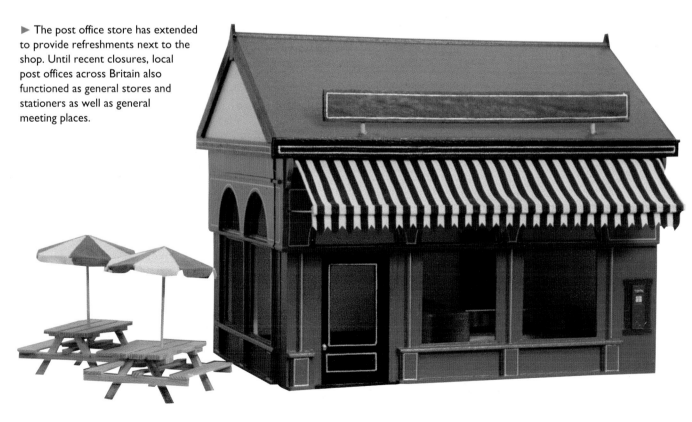

DESIGN A CAFÉ OR RESTAURANT IN A ROOM BOX

A room box, similar to those that I constructed or assembled from a kit for the store departments (pages 93 to 107), is also suitable for a café or restaurant. Plan what you want to include, then decide on the size you need.

It is not necessary to go to great expense to create an unusual setting. A mixture of high-quality craftsman-made pieces, together with some that are inexpensive to buy or that you can make for yourself, can be very satisfying.

CHOOSING MATERIALS

Start with the background. Choose a good variety of coloured cards and papers, including different textures, and play with them to see which look best together; sometimes, when you change the combinations, the effect will surprise you. Time spent on sorting out decorative materials and shifting them around to work out a scheme is well worthwhile. Colour and pattern can work together in many different ways; after thinking of a paper specifically as a wall covering, you may find that it would work far better as flooring, with something else for the walls.

Occasionally I have to reject a paper or card altogether, when I realize that my grand idea is not going to look good in its original form. Not everything works: keep an open mind and have the confidence to change your initial idea and move on. Sometimes, just using a pattern horizontally rather than vertically can make all the difference (see the Italian ice-cream parlour on page 131, where the horizontal stripes on the wallpaper look much more attractive than if the pattern had been used vertically).

◀ Decorative papers are the starting point for interesting restaurant decoration, in this case for an Indian restaurant (see page 148).

CHANGING THE LOOK

Colour is the single most important factor when designing a successful restaurant or bar: if you can get that right, everything else will fall into place.

The attractive restaurant corners that follow, demonstrate the great part that colour plays in altering the appearance of similar-sized rooms.

AFTER-DINNER COFFEE IN A GENTLEMEN'S CLUB

▲ Well-filled bookshelves line the walls of the library.

My first example is the comfortable, conservative setting of a gentlemen's London club. Many such clubs were established in the eighteenth century and have changed little since; patronized initially by the aristocracy, these were always exclusive. Even the grandest and wealthiest Regency bucks had to be proposed and approved before they were invited to become members, and to be refused because of some perceived flaw of character or irregularity of conduct was a dire fate.

Many such clubs still exist today, although they are more egalitarian. They are generally in grand London houses and always have a dining room and a library, but the gaming rooms of the eighteenth and early nineteenth centuries where, on occasion, entire estates were wagered on the turn of a card, are no more.

You do not need to include much furniture or many ornaments to create a comfortable, inviting room of this kind. Use a photocopier or computer to reduce the size of pictures of bookshelves, and paper the walls with them, taking care to make joins as discreet and neat as possible. Plan out the number of sheets you need and copy some spares before you start piecing them together, so that you do not have joins part way across books. If you prefer not to line all the walls with books, a dark green wallpaper would be suitable for some areas.

PRE-DINNER DRINKS CORNER OF A MODERN RESTAURANT

Equally simple but in complete contrast to the calm atmosphere of the gentlemen's club, the brilliant colours of the decorations in my second corner look stunning. We can assume that the main restaurant will be equally exciting as a venue for a special meal.

MAKE THE ROUND TABLES

For each table, you will need:

- 1¾in length of ⅜in diameter round wood dowel (45 x 10mm), for the pedestal
- 2in (50mm) diameter lid from a jar, for the table top
- 1in square of ¼in thick wood (25 x 25 x 6mm thick) for the base of the pedestal
- ½in square (12mm) piece of thin wood or card to glue to pedestal top and underside of table top

Glue together and paint with matt aluminium or metallic silver model enamel.

◄ A fuchsia-pink wall and one that is covered with mauve holographic giftwrap are balanced by a pale marble floor, partly covered by a suede rug (the reverse side of a leather sample).

MAKE THE BANQUETTE SEATING

The banquette seating can be made from three small boxes with padded fabric lids, each measuring approximately 2¾in L x 2¾in D x ¾in H (70 x 70 x 20mm). This type of inexpensive box is widely available from gift shops that stock Indian or African work, and in many colours and patterns. The soft, padded lid makes the seats look comfortable.

1 Draw a line precisely across the top centre of one box, complete with lid, and cut it in half, to provide two seat bases each 2¾in L x 1⅜in D x ¾in H (70 x 35 x 20mm). If you cut the boxes carefully with a craft knife, you will not damage the fabric covering. To prevent any tendency for it to fray, run a thin line of all-purpose glue along the cut edge.

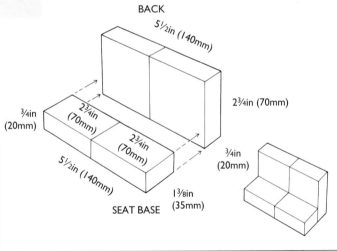

Make a banquette from three padded boxes

BACK

5½in (140mm)

2¾in (70mm)

¾in (20mm)

2¾in (70mm)

2¾in (70mm)

¾in (20mm)

5½in (140mm)

1⅜in (35mm)

SEAT BASE

2 Glue the 1⅜in (35mm) sides of the boxes together, to make a seat base 5½in L x 1⅜in D x ¾in H (140 x 35 x 20mm).

3 To make the seat back, glue the two remaining lidded boxes together, side by side.

4 To complete the banquette, glue the cut-open side of the seat base to the seat back.

VENETIAN RESTAURANT

► A romantic corner in my Venetian restaurant. On the side tables, the desserts are set out ready to serve. The gilded torchère is topped with golden glass flowers (a spray from a haberdasher's) in a decorative glass vase.

▼ The intarsia table features a swan centrepiece, and sorbets on a silver tray.

Venice is elegant, glamorous and romantic, and a candlelit dinner for two in a first-class Venetian restaurant will always be a memorable occasion. The myriad reflections of rippling water from the canal or lagoon outside would enhance the setting.

The use of a pale, textured wallpaper with a random pattern of small shiny squares gives the impression of reflections from water or candlelight, while a picture from a souvenir menu reproduces a view. Pictures of Venetian scenes are often shown in magazines as well as on postcards and greeting cards, so it should not be difficult to find something that would be suitable.

The eighteenth-century furniture was chosen carefully, and includes two cane-seated chairs that fit in well, although from an inexpensive range of period-style dolls' house furniture. Venetian glass is famed worldwide, so I decided to make a feature of my most treasured pieces of miniature glass. On the side tables, delicate tiered dishes for desserts are topped with flowers, while the rose-coloured glass candlesticks contain candles made of glass.

My room has a dark wood floor, but a stone floor would also be appropriate, with a carpet to soften the effect and provide warmth for the diners: Venetian palazzos can be very cold and damp, and some restaurants are in these former grand houses.

MODERN JAPANESE RESTAURANT IN A HOTEL

Although featuring the identical wallpaper and dark wood flooring, this restaurant corner could not be more different from the Venetian setting. The simple addition of black and red as the main accent colours is enough to change the ambience completely.

The finished scheme is striking, but the red banquette provides the only brilliant colour, so this corner looks a restful place to eat. The black-framed menu, a painting on the wall, and the slatted blind with the appearance of rattan are typically Japanese.

The low table is a box, painted black, with a top of black shiny card to simulate lacquer. The Japanese are so skilful at making miniatures from paper and card that it seemed appropriate to use similar methods.

With a single flower in a Kakiemonware porcelain vase on the table, other ornaments are unnecessary.

Japanese Food

Japanese cooking is an acquired taste for foreigners but is gaining ground in Western countries, where many leading hotels now have a Japanese restaurant on the premises, specializing in shabu shabu, sukiyaki or seafood nabe. If you are adventurous, you can cook your own food at the table, or – my own preference – have it prepared for you.

Fish, rice and green vegetables are the staples of Japanese food, so these are what should be shown in miniature scale. The table should be laid carefully, with plain white bowls and chopsticks (made from split and shortened matchsticks). Add paper napkins for a splash of colour against the black table top.

▲ A modern-style Japanese restaurant relies on a simple colour scheme accented in red and black.

▼ Fish is on the menu, and will be eaten with chopsticks from plain white bowls.

LUNCH AT THE GARDEN CENTRE

► The fish tank set into the wall is a picture framed in thick stripwood that is painted bright orange, to give it a three-dimensional appearance. Alternatively, for additional realism, you could use a miniature replica fish tank: these usually have 'fish' set into resin to give a watery effect.

My final examples are two contrasting restaurant corners that began with similar decorations, both featuring outdoor eating. Each restaurant has a brick wall behind the tables, but changing the floor from a simulated gravel in the first, to a bright red floor paper in the second, turns the outdoor daytime café into a terrace restaurant for evening dining.

Even non-gardeners usually enjoy garden centres. It is pleasant to wander around admiring the plants and flowers, and for serious gardeners there will also be a range of plant pots, urns, pebbles and flat stones for paths, as well as bulbs, bedding plants, shrubs and even small trees – all of which can be found in miniature scale. There may also be a section devoted to tropical fish, glass tanks and aquatic ornaments, and a play area for children.

Add as many plants and flowers as you wish, and provide some fresh vegetables for sale, and a corner for garden sculpture.

I used a dolls' house brick paper for the brick wall: remember always to choose a good quality, matt-finish paper, as some cheaper papers intended for children's dolls' houses are too shiny to look realistic. Alternatively, you can build your own brick wall, using real miniature bricks and grouting them in carefully, but remember that this will be a time-consuming process.

▼ The plain wooden table and chairs are an inexpensive set. Salad, pasties, fruit and bread rolls are typical garden centre fare, while juice and cola suit grown-ups and children. A self-service café can be indoors or outdoors. Mine has gravelled flooring of rough-textured, stone-coloured thick paper with round paving stones arranged as a winding, stepping-stone path to add further interest.

▼ The papers and cards that I chose to use in the garden centre. Remember to make a sign to fix on to the wall.

TERRACE DINING

Using the same brick wall as a starting point, the garden centre café is transformed by a deep red, textured paper floor to become a modern terrace restaurant, where a candlelit dinner is about to take place.

The two square tables are shown pushed together for a companionable meal, but could just as easily be used separately. They are made in a similar way to the round tables in the modern restaurant drinks corner (page 115) but this time are of wood.

▲ The table is assembled like this.

▲ The high walls of this outdoor restaurant corner will shelter the diners, so a candle on the table is appropriate. The large, modern, trompe l'œil light fitting suggests additional illumination.

▲ The black-and-grey ikat design on these boxes used to make the banquette contrasts well with the brick and the red floor. For extra comfort, the seat top is padded with ½in (12mm) thick black foam.

MAKE A SQUARE TABLE

You will need:

1¾in length of ⅜in diameter square wood dowel (45 x 10 x 10mm) for the pedestal

1½in square of ¼in thick wood for the table top (40 x 40 x 6mm)

1in square of ¼in thick wood for the base (25 x 25 x 6mm)

½in square (12 x 12mm) of thin wood to fit under the table top

1 Cut the wood to size and check with a set square that the top and base are square.

2 Stain the pieces before gluing them together, to avoid any possibility of smearing glue on to the wood before the stain is applied, as wood stain will only cover on bare wood.

3 Mark the centre of each square piece carefully.

4 Glue the ½in (12mm) square centrally to the underside of the table top to provide extra strength. Then glue the centre support to top and bottom.

EATING OUT – A GLOBAL TOUR

The restaurant corners shown on the previous pages illustrate contrasting decorative schemes that will provide a restful ambience for a quiet meal, or a more lively setting to put potential diners in a party mood. Colours that would not normally be considered for the home can look attractive in a public space, and striking arrangements are contrasted with more traditional schemes to show the possibilities.

To keep a historical perspective on dining out, my global tour begins in eighteenth-century style then continues with both formal and informal restaurants and cafés from around the world.

◄ This table is simple to make, and is suitable for modern cafés, restaurants or bars.

► The style of table and chair used in many French cafés and brasseries has become so popular that it is now commonplace in cafés and bars in many other countries.

In general, I have provided only two or three tables in the cafés and restaurants I designed and made for this book. This is sufficient in a single-room setting without overcrowding. Modern tables and banquette seating are easy to make, and you may want to include more – if you do, it is obviously more economical to make your own.

There is wide variation in styles and prices, from simple basic furniture that is suitable for modern settings, to the superior handmade furniture that is well worth saving up for to enhance a special project (see the French cafés on pages 127 and 129). Alternatively, furniture kits to assemble yourself are fun to tackle and also save money.

ECONOMY IDEAS

You can economize on some of the accessories, while splashing out on a few items that will take centre stage.

- Use plain white pottery if the plates are going to be mostly covered with food, or paint card plates.

- Buttons can also be used as plates and will look exotic, especially in oriental restaurants (see page 140).

- Choose sets of cheap wine bottles to fill a wine rack – but invest in two or three special bottles and some 'filled' wine glasses to place in full view.

- Make paper napkins from coloured paper or fine lawn.

- Note that even 'gold-plated' cutlery is inexpensive in dolls' house size.

- A small 'silver' lid from a bottle of perfume can be used as an ice bucket. Fill it with 'crushed ice' (glass from car windscreens that cannot cut you – it is usually easy to find some) to surround a bottle of champagne. Lids from some slightly larger containers (such as hand lotions) can be used as bar stools (see page 151).

- Chopsticks can be made from matchsticks – slice lengthwise and cut to length – one matchstick will provide two pairs of chopsticks (see page 117 and page 144).

- To add a touch of luxury, remember to put a vase on the table – even a single flower can look romantic.

DINNER IN A GEORGIAN ASSEMBLY ROOM

▲ Formal dining in the beautiful setting of a panelled Georgian-style room. In the eighteenth century, dinner was eaten at around four o'clock in the afternoon, so the background of Bath's Royal Crescent is viewed in daylight. It was only gradually that the time for dinner became later, so that eventually lunch was introduced to fill the gap between breakfast and dinner.

In the eighteenth century, elaborate meals of many courses were enjoyed on formal occasions. Wine was served in much smaller glasses than we use today, but the 'puddings' or dessert course could be spectacular. Tables were decorated with fruit and floral arrangements, often set out in a row along the centre of the table, or in the case of a smaller table, a pretty basket of fruit or flowers would be the centrepiece. In the spa town of Bath, south-west England you can still dine out in Georgian surroundings, as so many of the original buildings – including the Pump Room – are now used as cafés and restaurants.

Here, I have presented the dinner in a large, panelled room box that has a rear 'corridor' at the back, behind the windows. The walls are decorated in a greeny-blue – a very popular colour in the eighteenth century – which came from one of the historic paint ranges now reproduced by several paint manufacturers. There are no curtains to distract from the view of Bath's Royal Crescent that I have used as a backdrop behind the sash windows.

The food and the flower arrangements were all made by a professional miniaturist who has studied historic food; one of her specialities is dishes that are correct for the Georgian period. Each table has elegant china, serving dishes and plates, Georgian-style drinking glasses and, in the case of the more elaborate table – placed near to the fireplace, as Georgian rooms could be chilly – gold cutlery is set out.

▼ Dessert wine and fruit are set out on a side table, together with an elegant candleholder with space for a floral arrangement.

▲ A set of gold-patterned china is complemented by gold cutlery, while the punch bowl, complete with a set of glasses, is the centrepiece.

▲ Plainer and more robust fare – but equally appetizing – is served on a table reserved for a local squire and his family.

There is a definite class distinction in this assembly room. The food on the main table is spectacular, while the other, perhaps laid for a country squire and his guests, has roast beef rather than the more elaborate dishes on the first table. Precedence was very important, and manners formal.

A Table for Two

In a smaller room, you could arrange a table for two diners and imagine that they were making a stop on a journey. Travellers of any importance arranged for a private dining room when they stopped for a meal, and never mingled with the ordinary stage-coach passengers at a coaching inn. For this scenario, the room could be quite small, panelled in stained oak rather than the fashionable blue-green in the assembly room, and the furniture would be plainer. Pewter candlesticks would be suitable, and perhaps a small posy of flowers on the table in a jug, rather than the formal arrangements in my scene.

Panelling a Georgian Room

Panelled walls can be simulated by wallpaper, and very convincing dolls' house papers are available (see page 71). Alternatively, you can buy a kit to make up a room box together with a panelling kit to complete the walls with wood panels. Choose a historic colour in a matt or semi-matt finish or use oak wood stain for a simpler room.

The floors should be planked and polished to a soft sheen, never a glossy finish. I completed the ceiling with an embossed dolls' house ceiling paper, which I painted – like the walls above the panelling – with an off-white emulsion.

► The panelling provided in this kit is carefully designed to fit round the windows, door and fireplace that are provided. A shelf below the cornice is deep enough to hold plates or vases.

VISITORS' TEA ROOM IN A STATELY HOME

After the Second World War, many stately homes in Britain began to suffer from lack of funds and, to help with their upkeep and in order to stop them quietly crumbling away, ever more were opened to the public for a modest charge.

Visiting such an ancient house, especially one belonging to a member of the aristocracy, is a favourite weekend pastime in Britain, both for residents and tourists. It can be especially rewarding for the miniaturist, who can see original period decorations and beautiful furniture, portraits, silver and table settings that are sometimes arranged as though for a grand dinner party. We are able to take notes, buy postcards and guidebooks that show the rooms and give the history of the house or castle, and gather information that we can turn to good use for future projects.

No visit is complete without some refreshment, and tea is often available, generally in the former kitchen or housekeeper's quarters, or in an adjacent garden room or old stables. The National Trust in the UK has taken over and preserved many ancient buildings, and is particularly good in this respect.

One of my dolls' houses is a rather grand-looking castellated tower, and it boasts a sculpture court on the entrance floor (see below). This makes an interesting, if rather unusual setting for a visitors' tea room. There is enough space for two tea tables and an assortment of cakes and biscuits that look delicious. For the table settings I used plain white china, not his lordship's best porcelain.

▲ Remember to put a sign on the door to indicate opening hours. This is better done by hand rather than by simulating professional signwriting.

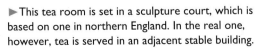
► This tea room is set in a sculpture court, which is based on one in northern England. In the real one, however, tea is served in an adjacent stable building.

Tea-time Food

If one of your skills is making food from a modelling compound such as Fimo, you might like to provide the food yourself. In my example the model food is bought – cakes and biscuits are always available from dolls' house shops or mail order outlets.

Rather than the lofty surroundings of my sculpture court, a tea room could be set in any period house that has a large Georgian or Victorian kitchen, or in a room box arranged as a plain, former servants' hall. The more conventional kitchen idea for a setting offers a good opportunity to include a dresser loaded with copper pans or a matching dinner service.

The tables and chairs should be plain, although the pottery can be decorated if you wish; a set of flower-sprigged or blue-and-white china is sometimes used. Some simple flower arrangements and a longcase clock would also enhance such a scene.

▼ Tea time may no longer be recognized as a meal in British homes, but a traditional tea is still regarded as a great treat when going out.

FRENCH CAFÉ

This café is arranged in a French shop similar to those shown on pages 79–89, and exterior decoration procedures were the same. It is slightly smaller than the other two, as the ground floor measures only 13¾in W x 8in D (350 x 205mm), with a ceiling height of 9in (230mm). I chose it because the façade resembled a French café I had visited in Paris. It is just large enough for three tables of different sizes with seating for five diners, and two more tables where the food and wine are laid out.

Unlike the equally distinctive English tea room, a French café is licensed to serve alcohol at any time of day, with or without a meal. It can also be a bistro or brasserie, and as such has always been a meeting place patronized as much by locals as tourists. So you need to decide whether you would like to reproduce a typically urban eating place like mine, or a village café that will be more rustic, slightly shabby but distinctively user-friendly. This would be the sort of place where everyone is greeted by name and a handshake, and where the old men of the village sit for most of the day playing cards or board games over a glass or two of the local wine.

▲ Blue and white is probably the most popular colour scheme for the façade of a French shop or café. Any shade of blue is permissible, from this bright mid-blue to a deep navy. Lace blinds at the windows protect the customers from the glare of the sun in the daytime, and provide some privacy to evening diners.

► To complete my French café, I found a realistic light, with fan blades that turn, from an inexpensive range of dolls' house lighting, and an etched glass screen to make a division in front of the door at the rear. The jugs for sweet peas on each table are of French-made stoneware.

▲ The menu on the wall is from an advertisement for a French restaurant chain, while the poster evokes 1920s Parisian café society. This table displays the main courses on offer – and, of course, wines.

▲ A tall stand for coats, hats and umbrellas is almost obligatory, as is a metal or wooden wall rack to hold newspapers. I bought French newspapers (in England) and photocopied them down to a suitable size – but you could also do this by using a scanner and computer.

Some Parisian cafés are very grand, especially those designed in the eighteenth century, when coffee drinking first became popular in France; others are more like drawing rooms, with velvet upholstered seating and gilded decorations, although in such a small building it is probably better to reproduce a less ostentatious style.

Planning the Café and Decorations

A café needs interesting decorations to please its customers. Like the traditional French shop, a tiled floor is almost obligatory. I chose blue-and-white tiles, but for a more rural establishment, brown and cream or red and green would be more suitable, and all these colour combinations are available in plasticized tile sheets.

Essential Furniture

The way the tables are arranged gives the café the nicely crowded air of a popular place to eat and drink. The bistro furniture is in the

▲ Irresistible desserts look typically French but were made by an English miniaturist. They include profiteroles, a choux pastry pyramid and a basket of cherries.

predominant style of such cafés, with the bentwood chairs that were an immediate success in the nineteenth century when they were patented by Thonet, and are still made and used today. These miniature versions are by a Belgian maker.

CAFÉ IN A CONSERVATORY

My second French café/brasserie came about when I bought a large, ready-decorated conservatory. It had a black-and-white tiled floor, which tempted me to continue this theme. I have enjoyed meals in conservatories restyled as restaurants, and this seemed the perfect opportunity to arrange a miniature version. The conservatory needed no additional decoration and features similar furniture and food to the small café – but there is more of both.

▼ The blue-green paint colour is one of my own favourite shades and is a good choice for the exterior and interior woodwork. The conservatory measures 18in W, 13in D and 19in H (460 x 330 x 480mm), with enough space for more tables and chairs than in the small café.

◄ The only opening into the conservatory is through its glazed double doors, so that great care was necessary when arranging the contents. The doors are fitted with brass working handles and bolts.

▼ The central display of flowers and a cherubic garden statue (previously used in the garden dining room, page 89), make a spectacular setting to greet diners as they arrive.

► There needs to be enough space for waiters to weave their way between tables and chairs, so it is important to plan exactly where these should be placed. Stained-glass panels throw coloured shadows on to the interior and provide an atmospheric setting for a meal.

ITALIAN ICE-CREAM PARLOUR

You do not have to live in Italy in order to enjoy Italian ice cream, which is always a top favourite with children and grown-ups alike. When I was a child, there was an Italian ice-cream parlour in the nearest town and later, when I moved to London, there was a similar family-run establishment nearby, which sold ices to take away or to eat in its pretty interior.

It was the most popular local venue for children's treats and birthday parties and, happily, it is still there, delighting a new generation of children.

This ice-cream parlour is set in the same room box that I used for the ladies' shoe department (see page 100). It is transformed by a pale, marbled floor and a striped wallpaper in ice-cream colours, giving a bright, summery feeling, while a blind at the window adds a vivid splash of colour.

For this setting, I made a card lining for the room box, leaving only one window showing, and covering the door, as I assume that the entrance is at the front.

▲ The pale, marbled floor and striped wallpaper (giftwrap) are true to Italian decorative style. The window blind, chosen to echo the strongest colour in the wallpaper, pulls the scheme together.

◄ This ready-made display unit holds wafers, sundaes and ice cream waiting to be served out. You might like to try making a freezer cabinet for yourself.

131

MAKE A FREEZER CABINET

1 For the base, use a box approx. 4in L x 2in D x 1¾in H (100 x 50 x 40mm), or make a base from card.

2 Paint the box sides – or cover them with thin, coloured card – and add some cut-out pictures of ice creams, and associated wording.

3 Glue a strip of very thin wood moulding just below the inside top of the box, to make a ridge for the lift-off lids to rest on.

4 Make the lids from three pieces of plastic window glazing, each approx. 1¼in W x 1¾in D (30 x 45mm), or to fit the size of your box. These will nestle side by side, resting on the inner ledge.

5 Cut three ¼in (6mm) long pieces of matchstick to make handles (or join two pieces into L-shapes, as shown below) and glue one on each lid, at the end nearest to the server.

6 Use three plastic or rigid paper containers, such as the shaped plastic liners from boxes of chocolates, to hold the ice cream in the freezer cabinet. These can be cut out to make individual containers that will fit in neatly.

7 Mould an uneven mound of modelling compound inside each container, making it lopsided as though some ice cream has been scooped out. Harden in the oven, following the instructions on the pack, and paint in colours to resemble strawberry, chocolate and vanilla ice cream.

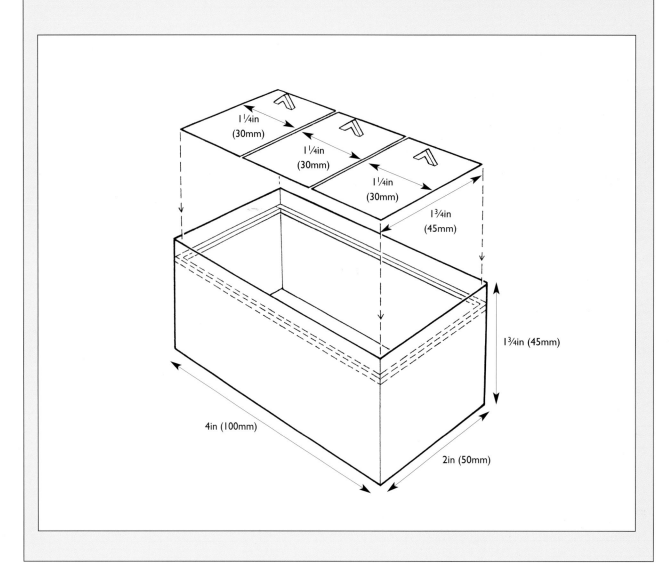

► The completed freezer cabinet, finished off with cut-out pictures of ice creams and a logo. The giant ice-cream cornet advertising sign I used is a plastic toy – a 'walking' ice cream that can be set in motion.

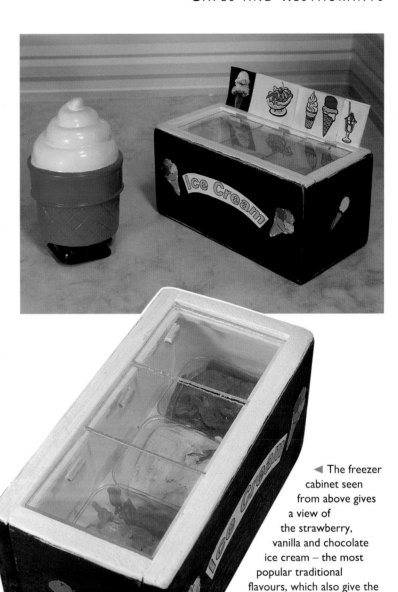

MAKE WAFERS

1 Cut a piece of ⅛in (3mm) thick wood into ⅜in (10mm) lengths.

2 Paint the sides and ends cream colour to resemble vanilla ice.

3 Paint thin card in a biscuit colour, cut to cover the top and bottom of each wafer, and glue in place.

MAKE CORNETS

A small display stand for cornets can be made from stripwood. Make the top from thick card or foamboard and punch holes through to take the cornets. Very neat fingers are needed to make ice-cream cornets, as this is extremely fiddly. However, it can be done, and gets quicker with a little practice!

1 Paint some cartridge paper biscuit colour and cut into pieces about ⅜in W x ⅝in L (10 x 16mm).

2 Roll the paper into a cone shape, taking care with the point at the bottom end, and fix with a dab of glue.

3 Make the blob of ice cream to top the cone from modelling compound, extending the lower edge so that it will fit inside the cone. When it is dry and painted, glue this in place.

◄ The freezer cabinet seen from above gives a view of the strawberry, vanilla and chocolate ice cream – the most popular traditional flavours, which also give the best colour contrast. As well as the ice cream in the freezer cabinet, you might like to make some wafers or cornets to display separately or to use on the tables for the customers.

133

SPANISH COFFEE LOUNGE
WITH A MOORISH INFLUENCE

▲ The colourful sunset (a picture taken from a magazine advertisement) is framed in wood moulding that is stained dark, to create an evening view.

Spain has a very individual style, its own special cuisine, and wonderful wines, but I decided to concentrate on coffee rather than the wine. I based this coffee lounge on some pictures I had seen in the travel section of a newspaper, featuring a superior hotel in southern Spain, where there is a strong Moorish influence.

Shortly afterwards I made a chance find in our local charity shop – an elegant miniature metal coffee pot, black with delicately incised silver decoration. It measures 5½in (140mm)

tall, and I imagine must have been brought home from Turkey or Morocco as a tourist souvenir. Subsequently, while looking through a book on restaurants, I found a picture of a restaurant that has a huge coffee pot – very similar to the one I had acquired – on the central staircase.

I imagine the real one must stand about four feet (1,220mm) tall and, placed on a plinth, it dominates the space. So my unusual find, transposed to southern Spain, was ideal to create a focus for my miniature scene.

◀ The pewter
candlesticks are
handmade and have
a duller finish than
the polished pewter
coffee pot and cups.
The cushions are
more ornamental
than comfortable,
but soften at least
the appearance of
these soapstone seats.

The colours shown here were used in the Spanish hotel. Black-and-white-tiled dolls' house paper is ideal for the floor, while the back wall is a thick, rough-textured, light stone paper. The side walls are both in a warm pink tone, one using marbled art paper and the other a rough mottled paper. Painting the walls would be equally successful.

The tables are padded box lids in ochre ikat fabric, similar to those used for banquettes in the restaurant corners on pages 115 and 119, but larger. The box bases are black, and can be used elsewhere as wall units or tables. The low seats are six-sided soapstone candleholders placed upside down, and the cushions are trimmings from a haberdashery department.

◀ Small bowls are placed on each table for the tapas that are always provided in Spain. Couscous is ideal to use for this purpose, as it will look like nuts.

135

I have included one green plant in a copper pot in my setting; large pottery urns or pots with tall plants or cacti with green or stripy leaves would also be suitable. You can make these from green plant ties: simply decide on a suitable width and shape the end to a point.

To make a feature of the coffee pot, or whatever you choose – a large ceramic jar would work well – you will need to provide a plinth of some kind. A stepped dais is useful, so that other, smaller ornaments can be displayed on the lower steps.

MAKE A STEPPED DAIS

You will need some 1in (25mm) thick balsa. Unlike solid wood, balsa is easy to cut but it does have the disadvantage that it will not take paint or stain well, so it needs to be covered.

1 First make the steps, by cutting three pieces of the balsa as follows:

    Lower step: 3in W x 3in L (75 x 75mm)
    Middle step: 2in W x 3in L (50 x 75mm)
    Top step: 1in W x 3in L (25 x 75mm)

2 Glue the three steps together to form the dais.

3 Cut ¼in (6mm) thick card or wood to cover the sides.

4 Cut fake leather, suede or felt to cover the top of each step and the sides of the dais and glue in place.

If the unit is to be placed against a wall, it is unnecessary to cover the back. However, it gives a neat finish if you do, and offers the further possibility of placing the unit in the main part of the room with the back showing.

► The stepped dais is an effective base for my ornamental coffee pot.

Make a stepped dais

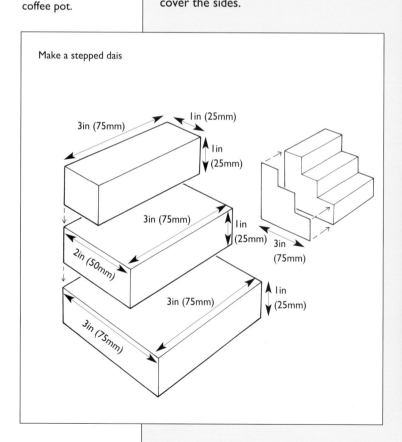

LUNCH IN A SYDNEY CAFÉ/BAR

Sydney is a perfect holiday destination but, if we are unable to take a vacation there, we can miniaturize the setting for an Australian meal. Sydney has an outgoing, lively environment, with plenty of fresh air and open harbour views, and for my café/bar I wanted to make a light, clean, modern setting, with clear bright colours and watery reflections to simulate the harbour beyond. I used a room box approximately 15in W x 11in D (380 x 280mm). Instead of painting the walls, I have lined them with white, coloured, and transparent card and acetate. Using transparent acetate over white on some of the wall surfaces adds a reflective glimmer. Both side walls are completed with white corrugated card to emphasize that this is the way in and out.

To provide a variation on the standard rectangular room, the back wall is curved slightly at the left-hand end, as a reminder of the waves outside – an easy effect to achieve, but fit the flooring first.

▲ To give a watery effect to emphasize the harbourside position of this café, the floor is of green card with a swirly pattern, covered with shiny green acetate.

MAKE A CURVING BACK WALL

1 Cut some coloured card long enough to cover the back wall and part of the side wall.

2 Then, starting at the right-hand end, glue the card along three-quarters of the length of the back wall. Curve it around the corner without fixing and glue the remainder to the side wall. Use a strong glue to make a permanent bond.

▼ The table is laid for two adults and two children, who will share a lobster platter. Soft drinks cartons and smaller plates are provided for the children's meals.

The inexpensive white table and chairs are enlivened by covering the table top with bright pink card, which is also used for the wallboards for the menu and also the restaurant logo. This is a self-service café, and the brief menu is written clearly using a fineline black pen on lined paper. The cashier's computerized till at the end of the counter is wood, painted with aluminium model enamel, while the modern designer stool is a square of Perspex fitted to a metallic cap from a perfume bottle.

This L-shaped counter is similar to the one used in the food hall (see page 106 for instructions and diagrams showing how to make one). However, this time I chose a brilliant turquoise mountboard to cover the base box and use as a counter top. In general, when using any board or card to make a table or counter top, I recommend colouring the white edges with a pencil crayon or fibretip pen to match or tone with the colour. In this modern setting, however, the edge has been left uncoloured to simulate white trim and to match the style of the white table with its bright pink top.

▲ An array of appetizing dishes is laid out on the counter. The food should include fish and salads as well as fresh fruit. Soft drinks and lagers are arranged in transparent plastic boxes that make realistic cool units.

▼ Many different types of card, acetate and paper combine to make the Sydney café fresh and appealing.

THAI RESTAURANT

▲ These exotic decorations create the right ambience for the restaurant, without the need to include much furniture. The low bench seat, which suits the height of the tables, is a box that contained jewellery.

I have only occasionally eaten in a Thai restaurant, although they are very popular and can be found in towns and cities worldwide. Each time, I have found it a thoroughly enjoyable experience. Quite apart from the delicate flavours of the delicious food, the quiet atmosphere and careful, attentive service in most Thai restaurants are a pleasure in themselves. The whole experience starts with the bringing of a warm, damp, scented towel to wipe your hands.

The care taken with the decorations is also a pleasure and guaranteed to delight the most discerning diner. There are usually some jewelled ornamental figures, or perhaps a gilded Buddha on a pedestal: the colours are muted, but with striking motifs, and the furniture may be of bamboo or rough-looking dark wood.

Start with the Colour

This ethnic restaurant idea began with the purple giftwrap which, after careful thought, I decided to use as flooring. I cut out some of the larger motifs and fixed them to the slightly rough-textured pinkish wallpaper to add to the exotic effect. The two low tables are of rough wood and bamboo; they came from our local department store and are intended to be used as soap dishes. I stained these darker to match the side table and covered the slatted tops with some thick woven paper samples.

◀ A contemplative Buddha presides over the meal. This gilded head came from a museum shop.

▼ The elaborate side table is a dolls' house miniature made in the Far East, with an equally exotic-looking flower arrangement on top.

It may be difficult to decide what food to lay out in a Far-Eastern restaurant. I solved this problem by using greenish pearl buttons as plates, with one turned wooden fruit on each to cover the holes. The natural wood colours of the fruit mean that it does not look as though Western apples or pears have been used, but something a little more exotic.

◀ The gold cutlery on the tables is rich-looking. Skeletal leaves (from a stationer's) make effective table decorations.

JAPANESE RESTAURANT

I have always admired Japanese art and ceramics, and longed to see Japan for myself. Finally I was able to go there, and loved it even more than I anticipated. Interestingly, apart from sushi which is now available in most Western cities, I did not especially like most traditional Japanese food. But I enjoyed both green tea and sake, and took careful note of the decor in the restaurants I visited in Tokyo and Kyoto.

A Private Room

My setting represents a private dining room in a typical restaurant, and the table is laid for two. When you enter a Japanese building through the door curtain, the custom is to remove your shoes when you step inside. There is sometimes another step up from the wooden floor to a raised area where the meal will be served and, to simulate this, I used a woven bamboo box. The floor cushions on either side of the low table provide the seating.

If you can't find a low enough table, one solution is to use an inexpensive one, shorten the legs and stain the wood dark. For my restaurant I was lucky enough to receive a gift in a small box with a simulated lacquer finish, and by making a few adjustments I found it made a very suitable table.

▼ An authentic Japanese restaurant exterior, made by a member of the Tokyo Dolls' House Club, complete with tiny garden below the window display.

Flower Arrangements

Westerners tend to think of Japanese flower arrangements in general as minimal, with one or three flowers arranged artistically in a small vase (the number 'four' is considered unlucky in Japan and odd numbers are always preferred to even ones). In public spaces such as hotels and restaurants, in Tokyo at least, there are huge and impressive flower arrangements that everyone stops to admire. I chose some exotic-looking flowers from the haberdasher's to fill a porcelain floor-standing vase to give this effect.

The Menu

Japanese restaurants always have the menu printed either outside or in the entrance, often with pictures or models of the food on offer, which is very helpful to visitors who do not speak Japanese. I assembled my menu board from several different sources, and reduced the resulting collage by copying it down to the right scale. It gives both the lunch and dinner menus.

▲ Background colours are muted, but the dull green wallpaper has glints of gold in the pattern. Entry is through a traditional dark blue curtain that screens the doorways of both restaurants and shops.

▼ The exotic flower arrangement is raised on a gold box plinth. The bamboo blind is a glass mat and the menu board is clearly printed and illustrated.

MAKE FLOOR CUSHIONS

To make floor cushions, fold a rectangle of fabric in half to make a square, insert padding of thin wadding and sew up the sides. Put a stitch right through the centre to make the cushion look squashy and comfortable.

▲ The model food in the Japanese restaurant window may be models in real life too, to show dishes on the menu to potential diners.

The Table Setting

The meal is served in plain white dolls' house china bowls. Make the chopsticks from short or cut-down matchsticks, remembering that Japanese chopsticks are shorter than those used in China. Split the matchstick lengthwise into two halves and then half again. Each matchstick will make two pairs of chopsticks.

The Food

I used chopped-up fine noodles in two of the bowls to simulate the very thick soba noodles served in Japan, and green and brownish dried herbs to represent miso soup. However, if you look closely you will notice that the rice in the large bowl is full size, as I had run out of sesame seeds (which work very well) when we took the photographs.

▼ The table is a shiny box that simulates a lacquer finish. A few Japanese lacquer miniatures add a note of authenticity to the setting.

CHINESE TEA HOUSE

I wanted to make this setting exceptionally delicate and pretty. The decorations were inspired by a beautiful shop with a Chinese influence close to my home and, with the shopowners' approval, I transposed their decorative theme to the tea house.

One special feature is the paintings of lotus blossoms on a pale wood floor. In the West, we are more likely to hang a painting on a wall, but it is worth considering a simulated floor painting, which will give a pretty and unusual effect. The wall frieze also adds a decorative touch.

▲ The floor is pink paper, the back wall is papyrus – to give a golden glint – from a stockist of art papers, and the other walls are white paper with a hint of pink.

▼ This table is placed on a lotus 'painting'. I have had the tea services used in my tea house for many years; they were handpainted on Chinese metal blanks, which are still made, but need to be decorated.

TO MAKE A WALL FRIEZE

Use giftwrap featuring Chinese teapots, jars and orchids to make a similar frieze. Cut out the relevant sections and copy down to a suitable size if necessary.

145

The tea house is arranged in the room box used earlier (as a Ladies Shoe Department and an Italian Ice-Cream Parlour), which has a double window at one end. Instead of fitting in the window frames, this time I decided to make an inner wall and cut out the window spaces. The openings are covered with a delicate, semi-transparent Japanese paper that has the appearance of fine voile but is much thinner and allows light to filter through.

A careful choice of materials is essential to achieve an unusual effect. Weight is important as well as appearance – in this tea room fragile papers and delicate fabrics as well as giftwrap gave the look I wanted. Look in stationers, haberdashers, gift shops, museums and stockists of art papers to find the perfect combination for your setting.

My original intention was that the tea house should serve only tea but I could not resist adding a stand with very pretty little cakes, despite being assured that traditional

◄ Appliqué motifs are attached to the blind; the delicate blue butterfly looks as though it is fluttering across.

▲ The selection of materials chosen for the tea house.

Chinese tea houses did not serve them. But soon after my tea house was completed and photographed, I read in a newspaper that a Chinese tea house had recently opened in Soho, London; the reviewer mentioned that it served the most delicious cakes he had ever tasted. So it seems that mine is a modern-style tea house.

INDIAN RESTAURANT

The first Indian restaurant in London – The Hindoostanee Coffee House – was opened in 1810 by entrepreneur Sake Dean Mahomed, an English speaker who had already written a book about his army life and subsequent travels. Since that time, Indian restaurants have enjoyed widespread popularity in England.

After-dinner conversation in this luxurious room would be enjoyable and relaxing. Gilded tea cups and a bowl of sweetmeats on the table are appropriate – the 'sweetmeats' here are actually red lentils.

My intention was to reproduce our friendly neighbourhood Indian restaurant – but a project does not always turn out as

originally planned. It has become much grander, influenced by pictures in a book on India showing a maharajah's palace that is now a hotel, which includes a room used for after-dinner tea and conversation.

To create a successful and convincing room of this type it is worth taking time and trouble to assemble an assortment of miniatures that will blend perfectly together. I used a mixture of English miniatures, Indian boxes, and incense burners from an ethnic gift shop. The carpet is a 1/12 dolls' house carpet, laid over a 'stone' floor of thick art paper. The Indian drum table and the ornamental elephant are both by English miniaturists, and the sparkling ornament on

▼ The jewelled paper on the back wall came from a supplier of art papers. It is soft and tears easily, so it took some care to fix it to the wall but the brilliant effect sets the scene perfectly.

◄ The low table and 'carved' pillars are of cast resin, from an inexpensive range of furniture that might not fit into the average domestic setting, but look absolutely right here. Even the deep yellow colouring suits this room. It is always worth considering something a little different for a restaurant scene.

a gilt stand is just right to represent the sort of jewelled 'toy' that might be present in such a flamboyant room; it is actually based on a Fabergé egg design, and also came from a gift shop.

It is worth remembering that much of the furniture still in place in the lavish palaces of India, whether private residences or those that have become hotels, often dates from the time of the Raj when Queen Victoria was Empress of India. Elaborate seating furniture and ornately carved side tables are still valued and enjoyed, while in England our tastes have become simpler. It would be perfectly correct to include period dolls' house furniture in such a room, whether Victorian or Georgian, when wealthy employees of The East India Company imported European furniture.

It is always worth doing some lateral thinking when choosing furniture for an unusual setting. Don't rely solely on the description of the piece in a dolls' house catalogue, but look carefully at the design and decide for yourself.

The chairs in the restaurant are from an inexpensive range of furniture available by mail order. They are based on a nineteenth-century design, but the unusual green of the upholstery with its Indian-looking motif and the curved back and legs reminiscent of Raj furniture, are appropriate for this room.

▲ The low table is a box with an inlaid lid from an ethnic gift shop, and is just the right height for the chair. The tea things on the table were gilded with a gold pen.

1930s BAR

▲ The Rainbow Room is a 1930s club setting inspired by Mood Indigo, a composition by Duke Ellington.

To complete this section on cafés and restaurants on a festive note, what could be better than a bar or club, where the decorations can be as imaginative as you are able to devise.

For this room, which recalls Hollywood films and nostalgic memories of scenes in *Casablanca*, the miniaturist chose indigo – a

deep blue with a hint of purple – for the banquette and the bar. The same shade is introduced as a border on the wallpaper, created by using a stamp and an inkpad from a craft shop.

The 1930s American club scene is very different from the traditional, comfortable pubs featured earlier (see pages 51 to 52), but

◄ The lighting effects are an optical illusion – there is no electric lighting in this miniature club.

the modern nightclub is an even greater contrast. Lighting is very important; in real life, designers rely on strobe lights that change colour at intervals to enliven the scene; in miniature size it is possible to simulate lighting effects by using silver fabric and sparkling papers. The trick is to start with a dark background colour and a very deep blue is often first choice in today's most up-to-date clubs.

THE BLUE DRAGON CLUB

The decorations for this club setting are planned on similar lines to a popular bar in California, where the sparkle of silver illuminates a midnight blue space. The paper used to establish the theme is an art paper with tiny, randomly placed silver sparkles.

The waterfall-effect behind the bar was cut from a lighting advertisement, while the right-hand wall is covered with shimmering silver fabric. The floor is giftwrap, again midnight blue with a pattern of shiny coloured circles in myriad colours.

► The 'spotlights' surrounding the bar are silver buttons with a diamante centre spot. The tables are easy to make (see instructions on page 115, where they were used in a modern restaurant drinks corner).

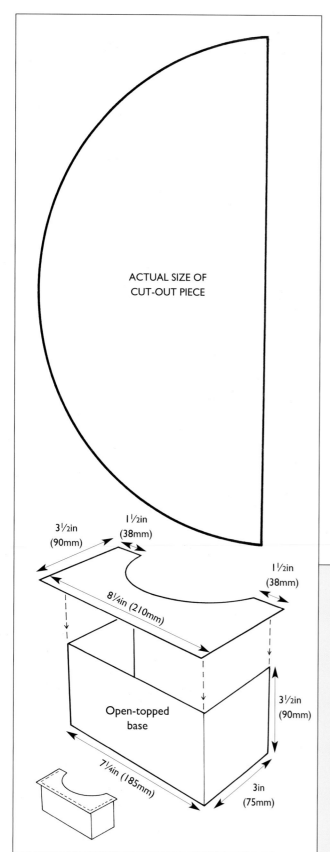

ACTUAL SIZE OF
CUT-OUT PIECE

3½in
(90mm)

1½in
(38mm)

1½in
(38mm)

8¼in (210mm)

3½in
(90mm)

Open-topped
base

7¼in (185mm)

3in
(75mm)

▲ The blue dragon that provided the name for my club is an iron-on motif. The pearl-strewn bouquet also came from a haberdasher's – the thin wire stems allow it to tremble slightly when used this way up, creating a freestanding, shimmering light effect.

TO MAKE THE BAR

My bar measures 7¼in L, 3in D and 3½in H (185 x 75 x 90mm). These measurements can be varied to suit your own setting.

1 Cut mountboard to the sizes given and glue the front and sides of the base together.

2 Cut out a D-shape from the bar top, for 'barman' at back (pattern supplied for cut-out, as used actual size).

3 Cover the sides and front of the bar with silver card and the top with shiny blue paper or card.

4 Glue the top to the base, so that the back edges are flush, but the top extends approx. ½in (12mm) around the front and sides. Add plenty of bottles and glasses – there is nothing like glass to add sparkle. And don't forget to put a bowl of nuts (couscous) on the bar top and on each table.

SUPPLIERS

Carol Black Miniatures (Mail Order)
Tel: +44 (0)1931 712330
Fax: (24 hours) +44 (0)1931 712990
Email: mail@carolblack.co.uk
(Colour catalogue available)

The Dolls House Emporium
Freephone: 0800 0523 643
Fax: +44 (0)1773 513772
Overseas Orders (including Channel Isles & Eire):
+44 (0)1773 514424
www.dollshouse.com
(Free colour catalogue)

Dolls' House Workshop
Tel: +44 (0)870 757 2372
Fax: +44 (0)870 757 2375
www.dollshouseworkshop.com
(Colour catalogue available)

J.S. Collins (Gable End Designs)
www. gable-end-designs.co.uk

Glenowen Ltd
Tel: +44 (0)116 240 4373
www.glenowendhf.co.uk
(Colour catalogue available)

Jackson's Miniatures Ltd
Tel: +44 (0)1747 824851
Fax: +44 (0)1747 821405
www.jacksonsminiatures.com
(Colour catalogue available)

Margaret's Miniatures of Warminster
Tel: +44 (0)1985 846797
Fax: +44 (0)1985 846796
(Colour catalogue available)

Caroline Nevill Miniatures of Bath
Tel/fax: +44 (0)1225 443091
www.carolinenevillminiatures.co.uk

The Original Dolls House Company
Tel: +44 (0)1435 864155
www.dijon.co.uk

Carl Schmieder Ltd
Tel: +44 (0)1398 332400
www.carlschmieder.ltd.uk

MAKERS OF FEATURED MINIATURES

Wendy Allin Miniatures: shell shop 34, toy shop 34, Sweets and chocolates 44.

Anglesey Dolls Houses: Annie's fruit and veg. shop 20, sweet shop 44, room box with glazed top 64, Georgian panelled room box 122.

Marie-France Beglan: patisserie with schoolchildren dolls 43, park kiosk with child dolls 49, child doll 73.

Elisabeth Bettler Causeret: French pottery 89.

Bonapartes: handpainted military models 70, 71.

Borcraft Miniatures: gilded wooden mouldings 86.

Box Clever Miniatures: Edwardian packaging 92 (top right).

Robert Bradshaw: artists' canvases and easel, palette 88 (bottom right).

Bygone Days: grand gilded sofa 86.

Carol Black Miniatures: window display 53 (top), (cranberry glass by Glasscraft).

Chapel Road Miniatures: sweet and tobacconist's shop 13 and 20 (left), shop and house 21 (bottom), market scene 51, The Trinity Arms 52, brewery and pub 52, traditional pub interior 52, greengrocer's window display 53, shop with signs 76.

Chicken Little Miniatures: wicker chair 85.

Delph Miniatures: hair salon 40, modern bar interior 52.

Derek Cliff: 'marble'-topped side table 122.

Christopher Cole: small Georgian shop 9.

Jeremy Collins: Tavistock chemist's shop 13, village stores and house 23, Sherbrooke pharmacy 27.

Jane Davies: child doll 75.

Delph Miniatures: hair salon 40, bar interior 52.

Dolls House Emporium: 'Marshall & Snellgrove' 12, Stratford market building 18, country store 23, chemist's display unit 27, ironmonger's 28, white showcase (florist's) 54, window display box 54, 55, 56 (top) 59, pizza place 111, cast resin chair 114, ornate side table 141, elaborate chair 148.

Dolls' House Holidays: shop 19, shops made by hobbyists 26, prototype shop for course work 26.

Dolls' House Workshop: sweet shop 8, antique shop 8, Tudor shop (and upper storey) 24, Arkwright's Tea Shop 110.

Elphin Dollshouses: corner shop 21, large corner shop 21 (decorated by Gill Green), Victoria Terrace 22.

Emily Art: carnival shop (*commedia dell'arte*) and lingerie shop 47, Belgian Christmas Market Stall 49.

Escutcheon: coffee table 114.

Karen Fitzhenry: rocking horses 75.

Bernd Franke: jeweller's and Bäckerei & Konditorei 46, German Christmas market stall 49.

Glenowen Ltd: The General Store 23, window display box 56 and 57, pagoda display unit 85.

Diana Gould: The Rainbow Room 150.

Ikuyo Hanami: Japanese greengrocer's 45.

Ann High: medieval merchant's shop 17.

John Hodgson: carved eagle console table 71, gilded picture frame, mirror and low table, Louis XV console table 86.

Tony Hooper: cast resin fireplace 86.

Imagine: Fred Ogden's shop 28, Bombay stores 38, handbag boutique 40, Pennies from Heaven and the Mackintosh Room 41, delicatessen 43.

The Ironworks: Indian drum table 148.

Jackson's Miniatures Ltd: spiral staircase kit 42, Georgian shop from plans 62.

Japanalia: lacquer furniture 143.

Lisa Johnson-Richards: children's clothing boutique 22, Edwardian couture gowns 39, Edwardian hats 58, Edwardian dresses and hat boxes 92.

Tony Knott: handmade pewter candlesticks 134, 135, 136.

Dominique Levy: china shop with majolica 30.

Lilliput Press: handmade and printed book 56.

Lincolns of Harrogate: grocery shop interior 15, Simpkin & James and cheese and cooked meats counter 42, mahogany shelf unit filled with bread and cakes 95.

Loi's Mini Treasures & Workshop: cheung-sam shop and workshop 37, 38.

The Luggage Lady: leather luggage 98, golfing set 99.

McQueenie Miniatures: case of duelling pistols 72, oriental bead curtain and corner whatnot 85.

The Mad Hatter: gentlemen's hats 57, 58.

Nicola Mascall: tapestry (needlepoint) cushions, firescreens, carpet, samplers, chair seat and back with footstool (chair and footstool by David Booth) 32, 33.

Merry Gourmet Miniatures: food and flower arrangements 122, 123, 124.

The Modelroom: Napoleonic gilded eagle table 71.

Vic Newey: Victorian street scene (arranged by Jean Amos) and street corner with lighting 50, Black Bear Tavern 51.

The Original Dolls' House Company: French-style furniture 89.

Pauline's Miniatures: food 127, 128.

Reutter Porzellan: armoire 84.

Timothy Richards: Michelin House model 93.

Zara Thomson Ribeaud: French-style baskets 31.

C & Y Roberson: metal newspaper rack 128.

L & A St Leger: carousel 57.

Rika Sato: rice cracker shop 45, Japanese delicatessen 45, Japanese restaurant 142, 144.

Sid Cooke Dolls' Houses: The Coxwold house and shop 24, Georgian shop kit and room box kit 63.

Stokesay Ware: blue-and-white china toilet set 54, 55.

Sue Cook Miniatures: swan table 85, Gothic mouldings and fireplace 125.

Tricia Street: porcelain figurines 55.

Susan Lee Miniatures: toys 56, shoes and slippers 59, gentlemen's boots 98 and 99, shoes and handbags 100 and 101.

Sussex Crafts: doorknobs 79, fireback and andirons 86.

Suzi Mac Miniatures: twist-stem round table 85.

Reg Thompson: glass candelabra 70, 71, glass candlesticks 86.

Tollgate Miniatures: Georgian shop from kit 67, two-storey Georgian shop (decorated and arranged by June Wright) 73, French shops 79, French café 127.

Tom Pouce: artist's easel and painting set 88 (bottom left), French bistro furniture and hat and coat stand 127, 128.

Toptoise: Mackintosh shop and flat 25, post office stores with café 112.

A Touch of England: French patisserie 15, Droguerie 29, majolica pottery on dresser 30, flower shop and lace shop 48.

Trigger Pond Dolls House: Tudor merchant's house with market space 18.

Warwick Miniatures: painted pewter toys and dolls' house 57, pewter and silverplated tableware 134, 135, 136.

Paul Wells: medieval guildhall and medieval shop 16.

Christina West: prototype of ice-cream freezer cabinet 133, display stand 133.

James Whitehead Miniatures: cello and lyre music stand 55.

Annie Willis: dog 73.

BIBLIOGRAPHY

Castillo, Encarno (Ed.)
Cool Restaurants Paris
TeNeues, 2003

Conran, Terence
Restaurants
Conran Octopus, 2000

Dietrich, Lucas (Ed.)
Style City Paris
Thames & Hudson, 2003

Draper-Stumm, Tara and Kendall, Derek
London's Shops: the world's emporium
English Heritage, 2002

Jitsukawa, Motoko
Contemporary Japanese Restaurant Design
Periplus, 2004

Morrison, Kathryn A.
English Shops and Shopping
Yale University Press in Association with English Heritage, 2003

Mostaedi, Arien
Design Bars
Carles Broto & Josep Mª Minguet, 2004

Mostaedi, Arien
Hotshops
Carles Broto & Josep Mª Minguet, 2004

Riewoldt, Otto
Retail Design
Laurence King, 2000

Scarr, Angie
Making Miniature Food and Market Stalls
GMC Publications Ltd, 2001

Taylor, Julie D.
Bars Pubs Cafés: Hot designs for Cool Spaces
Rockport Publishers Inc., 2000

ABOUT THE AUTHOR

Jean Nisbett began to take notice of period houses, their decorations and furniture before she was ten years old, and they have been a major interest ever since. While bringing up a family, she began working in miniature scale and has since developed an equal enthusiasm for reproducing modern architecture and design small scale. Her work has been shown on BBC Television, Channel 4, UK Style and TFI France.

She began writing while working in the London offices of an American advertising agency, and is well-known as the leading British writer on dolls' houses and miniatures. Her articles have appeared in specialist dolls' house magazines since 1985, and regularly in GMC's *The Dolls' House Magazine* since the first issue in 1998.

Jean lives in Somerset, south-west England, and this is her seventh book for GMC Publications.

INDEX

A
acetate sheet 66, 68, 97
adhesives 65
antiquarian bookshop 56
antique shop 35–6
artists' brushes 66
artists' mount board 96
artist's shop and studio 87–9
atmosphere, creating 50–1
Austen, Jane 19

B
bakery and cake shop 46
banquette seating 115
bar, making a 152
bar stools 121
bars
    Blue Dragon Club 151–2
    1930s bar 150–1
    see also pubs
basket shop 31
Bergdorf Goodman 94
bibliography 156
'bits' boxes 97
Blackie, Walter 25
blades 66
blinds, Rattan 83
Blu-tack 55
Blue Dragon Club 151–2
Bombay store 38
bookshelves, creating effect of 114
bookshop, antiquarian 56
Bostik 65
bottles 52, 121
boxes
    shell 34
    as shop fittings 96
brass-look letters 77
bricks 74, 118
brocante 83–6
brushes
basic kit 66
for narrow spaces 81

C
cafés 15, 112, 113
    café in a conservatory 129–30
    French café 127–8
    Sydney café/bar 137–9
carpet, flock paper as 100
chandeliers 84
chemists' shops 27
cheung-sam shop and workshop 37–8
china shops 30, 54–5
    gift and china department 102–3

Chinese projects
    cheung-sam shop and workshop 37–8
    tea house 145–7
chopsticks 121, 144
clothing shops
    Bombay store 38
    cheung-sam shop and workshop 37–8
    Edwardian ladies' clothing display 39
club, gentlemen's 114
colours
    historic paint ranges 69, 123
    for restaurants 114
commedia dell'arte shop 47
computers
    auction sites 62
    lettering technique 78
conservatory café 129–30
copyright 97
corner shops 21
cornets 133
cornices 66
counters, L-shaped 106
country stores 23
craft knives 66
crushed ice 121
cushions 143
cutlery 121
cutting mats 65

D
dais, stepped 136
decorating
    equipment 66
    materials 14, 113 (see also paints)
    slide-in room liners 96
delicatessens 42
department stores 92–7
    food hall 104–7
    gifts and china 102–3
    ladies' shoes 100–1
    sports and leisure 98–9
display boxes 54
display units 95
double-sided tape 96
Droguerie, The 29

E
Edwardian period
    ladies' clothing display 39
    shops 20–1, 92
emery boards 82
emporia 92
equipment
    for decoration 66
    for kit assembly 65, 66
Evostik 65

F
fascia boards 77–8
fibre-tip pens 97
Fimo 126
fish tanks 118
floor coverings
   carpet 100
   tiles 84, 128
   wood 98
flower and gift shop 48
food 107, 126
food hall 104–7
freezer cabinet 132
French projects
   artist's shop and studio 87–9
   basket shop 31
   brocante 83–6
   café in a conservatory 129–30
   The Droguerie 29
   flower and gift shop 48
   French café 127–8
   lace shop 48
   park kiosk 49
   ready-built shop 79–89
friezes 88, 145
furniture shop 41

G
garden centre lunch 118
general stores 23
gentlemen's club 114
Georgian period 19
   assembly room dinner 122–4
   single-storey shop 67–72
   two-storey shop 73–5
German shops
   bakery and cake shop 46
   Christmas stall 49
   jeweller 46
gift and china department 102–3
giftwrap 82, 96
glues 65
greetings cards 97
grocers' shops 42
guildhalls 17

H
hair salon 40
handbag shop 40
hat shops
   hatter's 57–8
   milliner's 58

I
ice bucket 121
ice-cream parlour 131–3
Indian style projects
   Bombay store 38
   restaurant 148–9
ironmonger's shop 28
Italian ice-cream parlour 131–3

J
Japanese style projects
   food shops 45
   hotel restaurant 117
   Japanese restaurant 142–4
   kiosks 49
jeweller 46

K
kiosks 49
kits 12, 63
   assembling 65–9
knives 66

L
L-shaped counter 106
lace shop 48
laundry markers 97
lettering
   computer technique 78
   pens for 97
   sources 76, 77
   stencilling technique 77–8
   for toy shop 57
lighting effects, simulating 151
lingerie shop 47

M
Mackintosh, Charles Rennie 25, 41
magazine cuttings 97
manufacturers 154–5
marble, faux 86
market crosses 16–17
market stalls 49
Matisse, Henri 88
MDF 64
medieval shops 16–17
military model shop 70–2
milliner's 58
mini-mitre box and saw 66
model enamel 97, 101
Monet, Claude 87, 89
mount board 96
music shop 55

N
napkins 121
needlepoint shop 32–3
newspaper cuttings 97
1930s bar 150–1

O
Ogden, Fred 28

P
paint brushes
   basic kit 66
   for narrow spaces 81
painting techniques 68–70, 80–3
   faux marble 86
   preparing plywood/MDF 64

paints 69, 123
    model enamel 97, 101
panelled walls 124
paper 113, 146
    brick effect 74, 118
    flock 100
    see also wallpaper
paper napkins 121
pens
    fibre-tip 97
    gold and silver 97
pharmacies 27
plans, building from 62
plants, making 136
plates 121, 141
plywood 64
pubs 51–2

R
Rattan blinds 83
rice 144
room boxes 63–4
    garden centre lunch 118
    gentlemen's club 114
    modern Japanese restaurant 117
    pre-dinner drinks corner 115
    terrace dining 119
    Venetian restaurant 116
rulers 65, 66

S
safety 66
scale 72
Scotch Tape 96
Scottish shop and home 25
screwdrivers 65
Selfridges 92, 94
set squares 65
shell shop 34
shelving units 95
shoes
    ladies' shoe department 100–1
    shoe shop 59
shop fittings 95
shop signs 59, 76–8
shops
    with living accommodation 24–6
sources 12–13, 62
shutters, painting 81

skirting boards 66
slide-in room liners 96
Spanish coffee lounge 134–6
sport and leisure department 98–9
staircase, spiral 42
stately home tea room 125–6
stencil lettering 77–8
stepped dais 136
storeys, adding extra 35
streets projects 22
suppliers 153
sweet shop 44
Sydney café/bar 137–9

T
tables
    low 142
    round 115
    square 119
tapestry shop 32–3
taverns 51–2
terrace dining 119
Thai restaurant 140–1
tiled floors 84, 128
tools and equipment
    for decoration 66
    for kit assembly 65, 66
toy shops 34, 56–7, 75
Tudor shops 18

V
Venice
    commedia dell'arte shop 47
    Venetian restaurant 116
Victorian shops 20–1, 75

W
wafers (ice cream) 133
wall friezes 88, 145
wall panelling 124
wallpaper 82, 96, 113
    applying 70–2
walls, curving 138
window display boxes 54
window dressing 53
windows
    acetate sheet 66, 68, 97
    painting 81, 82
wooden floors 98

GMC Publications
Castle Place, 166 High Street, Lewes, East Sussex BN7 1XU United Kingdom
Tel: 01273 488005   Fax: 01273 402866   E-mail: pubs@thegmcgroup.com
Website: www.gmcbooks.com
Contact us for a complete catalogue, or visit our website.
Orders by credit card are accepted.